Essential Home Security
A Layman's Guide
Stan Wasilik

ESSENTIAL HOME SECURITY

A Layman's Guide

Essential Home Security / A Layman's Guide
ISBN: 1453732039
EAN-13: 9781453732038.

With special thanks to Naz and Virginia

Table of Contents

CHAPTER 1
The Problem

Household burglary accounts for nearly one-in-five of all property crimes in the U.S.[1] Although many categories of crime have declined in recent years, this has not generally been the case with burglary. Both the incidence of burglary and the value of the property taken is staggering, and the statistics apply equally from the largest cities to the smallest towns. On a personal level, burglary victims experience more than a loss of property. Victims also endure lingering fear, a deep sense of violation, and acute vulnerability. Fortunately, we have tools to combat this insidious and persistent threat.

The incidence of burglary and the value of the property taken is higher now than ever.

This book provides an essential overview of the methods commonly used by those who want to make their homes more secure. While the content offers information for those who like to tackle projects around the house, it provides equal guidance to those who do not. Many of the measures apply whether the home is an apartment, townhouse, or single-family dwelling. The information is useful to young or old, to women or men, and to singles or large families, and an effort has been made to avoid jargon and unnecessarily detailed technical explanations.

The book offers a checklist to help you assess your situation, and covers appropriate physical measures, ranging from simple locks to complex alarms and surveillance systems. The publication goes beyond these concrete steps and highlights the

---

1   U.S. Department of Justice, National Crime Victimization Survey, Statistics Bulletin, December 2008, NCJ 224390

psychological and behavioral tendencies that limit the effectiveness of any structural security measures already in place.

The presence of quality locks, alarms, and other devices in a residence may provide a sense of security. Yet one of the gravest and most-often overlooked issues with home security systems and practices is that people *do not use* these systems and practices consistently. Some crime experts estimate that homeowners with active, monitored alarm systems fail to set those alarms more than half the time.

One of the gravest and most-often overlooked issues with home security systems and practices is that people do not use these systems and practices consistently.

the time. Mechanical and electronic security measures protect only if activated. Essential Home Security seeks to overcome attitudes or habits that lead to oversights in home protection. Vigilance remains a most powerful security tool.

Book Goals:

▶ You'll complete a detailed check of your current personal security situation. You'll understand what effective security measures you have or do not have in place.

▶ You'll understand the steps you may take to make your home a harder, riskier, and less rewarding criminal target.

▶ You'll understand how to implement these steps intelligently.

▶ You'll be aware of the behavioral tendencies towards complacency and understand the importance importance of avoiding it.

▶ You'll understand that few security measures are without drawbacks, and you will be better able to evaluate which measures are appropriate for you.

Book Overview:

►　**Chapters 1-2** offer general background and tips on best use of this book. A personal crime story illustrates how attitude and behavior affect security. The sections explain security apathy and suggest a method for preventing it. The approach attempts to simplify the process of examining and making security decisions that are right for you.

►　**Chapter 3** contains the ***Essential Home Security Checklists,*** designed to take a thorough inventory of your current level of home security.

►　**Chapters 4-15** offer detailed guides for implementing the steps included in the Essential Home Security Checklist.

►　**Chapter 16** briefly looks at security dogs and personal defense firearms. These items differ from the other measures described in this book for a number of reasons, including:

- Either measure may involve the implication, threat or use of bodily harm or deadly force.
- Both measures have criminal and civil liability considerations that vary significantly from state to state.
- These topics require extensive discussion. Many manuals specifically devoted to dogs or to firearms for the purposes of home security and self defense are available, and readers are urged to thoroughly research these topics before making security-based decisions.

CHAPTER 2
A Thoughtful Security Approach

Unpleasant Realities

In apartments, condominiums and single-family residences, criminals burglarize, rob and, in some cases, traumatize victims in the sanctity of their own homes.   Law enforcement agencies respond to crime; It's unrealistic to expect them to prevent it. You must participate in the protection of your home and property.

If you are a crime victim, you know too well the feeling of powerlessness, the sense of violation, and the anger and fear that can follow. Take heart, though, you are far from defenseless. You can dramatically increase your personal security if you take a number of simple, sustainable measures.

Unfortunately, it's *often only after* suffering a close call with crime, losing valuable property, enduring a traumatic situation or even a violent attack that most people take serious action. Fortunately, not all need follow this path. You can learn what crime victims often learn without experiencing personal trauma or loss. In fact, you can learn much more.

The National Archive of Criminal Justice Data (NCVS) indicates that *almost a third* of unlawful entries are unforced.[2] Burglaries routinely occur in households that have spent large sums on alarm systems, high-quality locks, surveillance systems and more. For some months, residents carefully set new alarm systems, lock doors, and take other measures, but over time may become less and less likely to do so.

---

2   U.S. Department of Justice / Office of Justice Programs / Bureau of Justice Statistics http://www.ojp.usdoj.gov/bjs/pub/pdf/cvus0604.pdf Table 59. Personal and property crimes.

Most homes have several security tools that are not used regularly or correctly.

Any good security manual warns you to lock doors and set alarms, and you've surely heard such advice from countless sources. You *know* you should lock your doors and set your alarms. Unfortunately, the knowledge alone is insufficient. You must change your behavior.   There is little point in spending time, money, and energy on security systems unless you give equal effort to consistent use. The advice in this chapter is designed to help maintain consistent security behaviors.

A Personal Crime Story

I lived in a nice section of Houston, Texas, for a little over five years. Many on my block lived there for twenty years or more; some grew up in the homes they now own. Surrounding areas prospered and changed, yet neighbors still gathered to visit on front porches in the evening. I felt safe, secure, and fortunate to be in such a setting. I had no idea that my sense of security was false. As safe as my home and surroundings seemed, I would discover that no neighborhood is immune to crime.

I knew my life depended on what would transpire in the next few seconds, but there was no time to make a well-reasoned decision.

On one particularly hot summer morning, I entered my living room after running out for a doctor's appointment. The house was quiet, my wife was at work, our son gone for the day. I noticed that my patio door was ajar and I chastised myself for leaving it open, perhaps when I'd stepped out to admire my garden earlier in the day. Or had I?

My question was answered before I'd walked to the door to close it. I heard quick footsteps behind me, turned, and was stunned to find myself little more than an arm's length away from a very large, powerfully built intruder -- an intruder who made certain I saw the gun tucked into his clothing.

My wife always harbored concerns about security. I didn't share her fears and would ask her, "what's the worst thing that could happen?" Over the years, I'd heard of a few incidents of petty theft in the neighborhood, but little more. I considered these rare, worst case scenarios thanks to our location. Now, as I faced an armed criminal caught-in-the-act, it became very clear to me the "worst thing that could happen" was well beyond what I had been willing to admit.

I watched the intruder draw a sawed-off shotgun and level it at my face. I instinctively inched my way closer to the open patio door, told him not to shoot and that he could take whatever he wanted. He ordered me to stop and told me to get on the floor. I knew my life might depend on what would transpire in the next few seconds, but there was no time to make a reasoned decision. I could only act and hope for the best.

My intuition said run, and run I did. I ran as I'd never run before and without a backwards glance. I ran out the jimmied back door, through the fence gate and down the street, dialing 911 on my cell phone as I sprinted. Fortunately, I was not shot in the back, nor did I suffer heat stroke or have a heart attack from the adrenaline rush combined with subjecting my middle-aged body to a long, hard run in 104 degree heat. I had been lucky, or so I told myself.

Bad Luck or Poor Inadequate Security?

In the weeks that followed, I became increasingly aware that I might have easily avoided the entire situation. I realized how lax I had become regarding security measures. I owned an alarm system, but I had not set it that day. I'd failed to use this critical device that might have frightened the burglar away or warned me not to enter the home. The intruder had easily entered by prying open a sliding glass door

I had replaced a few years ago, but had delayed restoring to the same bolt-locked security level of the original door. I'd intended to put vertical blinds on the door so that it wouldn't be so easy to see that my home was unoccupied, but hadn't managed to do that, either. I regretfully acknowledged that I was an easy mark.

While I had been "lucky" to escape without harm, a more accurate view of the event was that I had been lucky something like this had not happened sooner. I began to take stock of just how secure my home was and found more lapses and gaps than I care to admit. I was shocked. I'd lived in a crime-prone neighborhood in South Florida for many years and had been very careful about my home security. It hadn't been difficult; I'd just followed a safe routine and had simple measures in place. So how had I become so soft over the years?

Security Apathy

"Soft" as I had become, I wasn't cavalier about personal safety. My home was well lit, well kept, and equipped with a monitored alarm system. I knew my neighbors and we looked out for one another. We collected each other's mail and newspapers when someone was on vacation and took note of strange vehicles or activity. Why, then, was I so easily victimized? Because of our combined efforts, our neighborhood had been virtually crime free for some time. Gradually, I began to feel that the very things that kept me safe and prevented crimes really weren't that important. After all "nothing like that ever happens around here" seemed a very true statement.

We may gradually, passively, and unknowingly make ourselves more inviting crime targets.

In hindsight I realized that, as years went by, I began to set the alarm less frequently and often failed to activate it at night when I was home. I occasionally let my mail accumulate while I was away, sometimes for a week or more. I neglected the sliding glass door although I knew it was not secure. In effect, I relinquished some of the very tools that had kept me safe. The tendency to become lax and less diligent over time is, unfortunately, an all-too-common aspect of human behavior. The longer without incident or threat, the longer the "lucky streak" lasts, the less security conscious we become - often abandoning basic security defenses. We may gradually, passively, and unknowingly make ourselves a more inviting crime target.

Even when several crimes are committed in a supposedly "safe" neighborhood, behavioral change isn't assured; complacency tends to entrench. Following the incident in my own home, my neighbors talked about fixing old locks (but never did), they returned to leaving porch lights on at night (for a few weeks), and kept a close eye on strangers in the neighborhood (perhaps for a few months). Only after another series of burglaries took place in nearby homes were they fully aware that, they too, were vulnerable.

If you are a recent crime victim, you're probably keenly aware of your security measures and your behavior. For those of you who are more fortunate, please use the method described in the following section - or any method that works for you - to stay vigilant.

Fighting Complacency

How do you avoid complacency or security apathy? If the behaviors described are so prevalent and seemingly biologically ingrained, is it possible to prevent them?

It is possible to maintain vigilance, and the first step is to understand the mental states that relate to personal security.

Most of us go through our days in one of two mental states:

1. Relaxed but alert and aware of surroundings

2. Relaxed and unaware of surroundings

If a threat is introduced, the progression from each of these states is very different:

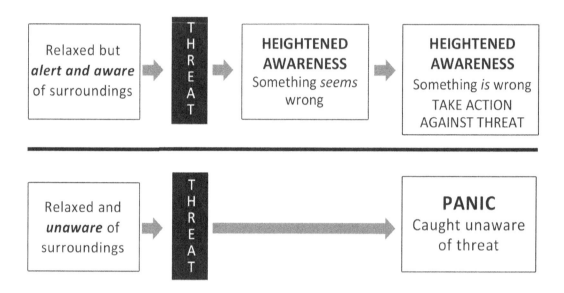

These mental states are generally used to describe behavior outside of the home, but they are pertinent to home security. Why? Because you are most likely to be in the "unaware" state in the safety of your own home. Many basic home security measures such as alarm systems and motion-activated lighting work because they warn of threats. They are designed to move you from the "unaware" state to "aware" or "heightened awareness" *before* you face an imminent, proximate threat and enter a panic state.

One simple method designed to combat complacency follows, and consists of three steps:

1. Ask yourself a question.

Begin with a simple, behavioral self-check by asking yourself this key question:
In places such as your own home, are you currently less aware and vigilant of personal security issues than you have been in the past?

Regardless of the specific measures, systems, or routines that you have in place, this question should be easy to answer. If you have any doubt, simply answer "yes."

2. Modify your behavior

If you answered "no," that you consistently employ the security measures at your disposal, move to step three. However, if you answered "yes" or "uncertain," regarding your security practices, take the following steps:

▶ Review the Security Checklists in Chapter Three. Compare your situation and behavior against the checklist.

▶ If you have security measures that you are not using consistently or correctly, *begin or resume doing so now*.

▶ If there are security measures on the checklists you have intended to implement but have not, take immediate action or, at least set a near-term deadline for yourself (one you'll adhere to) to implement these measures.

▶ Finally, if you live with others, discuss the lapses in security and have everyone commit to immediate action and an immediate end to the apathy.

Lack motivation? Re-read the personal crime story in this book and the surrounding sections. Think about what caused you to read this book in the first place. Watch the local news and remember that crime is not confined to "someone else." Speak to a local police officer about the importance of security in your neighborhood. You needn't terrify yourself. Just do whatever is necessary to get you to take these steps.

3. Set a Reminder

The risk of a gradual return to carelessness is strong. It's important you continue to ask the key question, at minimum, every few months. A "mental note" is insufficient. Set a automated reminder to work the three steps all over again.

It's best to use the same method you use to remind yourself of other important events such as doctor's appointments or birthdays. Make an appointment for yourself in your cell or smart phone, your PDA or personal organizer, your calendar or any other place that you check routinely or provides an auto-alert.   The important factor is to insure that you will be well aware of reminder.

Set these appointments at least quarterly and as far into the future as you can. Label them "Security check" or whatever description you like, but it's best to be consistent and to be sure the purpose of the reminder will be clear to you.

When the reminder is triggered, simply return to step one and ask yourself the critical question once again.

Security: How Much is Enough?

How wonderful it would be if there were a 100%, surefire way to prevent break-ins or other crimes. It's not possible, of course, to foresee and prevent all negative situations. What, then, is a reasonable approach? How many security steps can or should you take? How much can or should you spend? There are hundreds of measures, ranging from simple locks to remote home surveillance and control systems to ten foot, wrought iron fences surrounding your property. Each has a purpose, a cost, benefits, and drawbacks.

Just as a gambler in Las Vegas makes betting decisions to increase the odds of winning at blackjack, you can take actions that increase the odds of avoiding crime. Each action tips the odds just a bit more in your favor. Insurance companies certainly play the odds. They know that you are statistically less likely to lose property if a monitored alarm system is in place, and often give a corresponding discount on your homeowner's or renter's insurance premium.

How do you decide which measures give you comfort and security at a price you can afford? Start by taking several steps to assess your personal risks and specific security needs. You can't make intelligent, personalized home security choices without the context these steps provide.

A Reality Check - Assessing Geographic Risk

Before you lock-in on a budget, it is important that your planned sense of "comfort" doesn't rely on a false sense of your environment or on a hazy picture of what you stand to lose

First, become informed about the crime risks in your apartment complex or neighborhood. In the hours following my confrontation with an intruder, police mentioned a nearby "crime alley." I'd not heard the term and asked the officer to explain. He pointed out that a large series of run-down apartment complexes, about ten blocks south of my neighborhood, were notorious for drug, gang and other criminal activity. To the north, transitional neighborhoods painted strange and incongruous pictures. Expensive, newly constructed homes and poorly maintained, ramshackle structures stood side by side. High-end retail stores shared strip malls with pawn shops and check cashing outlets. Shoppers wore extravagant jewelry and clothing while the homeless or destitute begged for coins just yards away. Police considered the main thoroughfare that connected these disparate populations and neighborhoods to be a well-worn pathway of criminal activity. Had I been aware that my seemingly insulated location was adjacent to a high crime corridor, I might have been more active in protecting my home.

Become informed so that you understand any high-risk situations in or near your neighborhood. Crime reports for by neighborhood are available online in many cities. Additionally, your local police bureau usually can offer an accurate picture of the type and frequency of crime in your area.

Consider your living situation. Do you live in an apartment complex where neighbors rarely know one another and strangers can freely enter and roam the property? Do you live in a home with few security measures? Do you have a watchdog? Don't fall into the trap of assuming the crimes reported in the newspaper or on the nightly news only happen elsewhere. Many simple burglaries don't make the nightly news-casts, especially in large metropolitan areas.

Take Stock and Protect What's Important

Second, take a reasonable inventory of your household, estimating the replacement cost for high-theft-risk belongings such as laptops, flat-screen TV sets, jewelry, guns and other portable, valuable items. This is also a good time to photograph or video-tape possessions, record serial numbers, and mark valuable property with an electric engraver or invisible ink: sound security steps described in detail in Chapter 13.

You may own more high-risk belongings than you thought.

You may find you have far more invested in high-risk belongings than you thought and decide more protection is both necessary and well worth the cost. Sadly, personal injury, psychological trauma, and loss of life do occur during illegal home entries and it is impossible to place a dollar value on these events. However, if you ascertain the value of your belongings and consider your living situation (Do you have children or loved ones living with you?), you'll have a better perspective as you make determinations about your security budget and about how you can best allocate it.

Examples:

> ▶ If you have children, you may choose to put more security measures into place than if you lived alone, and more measures that directly protect your children. You may wish to install alarm sensors on all windows in children's bedrooms. You might locate a panic button in a central area that children can reach quickly. You may even consider a safe room.

> ▶ If you are often away from home and have many valuable, hard-to-replace items that you cherish, you may invest in automatic light timers or more sophisticated systems in order to make it hard for an intruder to tell that the home is unoccupied. You might ask neighbors to gather accumulating flyers or newspapers that give away a resident's absence.

> ▶ If you have irreplaceable documents, jewelry or other items, you might consider installing a home safe or, better yet, a safety deposit box at your local bank.

> ▶ If you live alone and your area is prone to violent home invasion, you may wish to focus on alarm sensors that give you warning *before* intruders are inside the home, such as window-screen alarm sensors. You may opt for burglar bars or security grates, or even decide that a guard dog or personal firearm is an appropriate choice for you.

Remember that each action adds some degree of protection, so even one or two measures are better than none at all. Your goal is to enact the best defenses you can afford in the places where you have the greatest security concerns.

CHAPTER 3
Essential Checklists

Identify the Goals

A common argument in home security discussions is, "If thieves really want to get into your home, they're going to get in no matter what you do."

Suppose that statement is true. A thief who wants to get in can and will? If so, that's helpful knowledge, as it clarifies the objective. If thieves can break in whenever they want to, it's important to ensure that they don't particularly want to break in to your home.

If thieves can break in whenever they wish, it's important you make sure they don't want to break in.

This is not as difficult as it sounds. Most burglars are amateurs looking for a quick and easy target. They may lack the tools or abilities to break into a home that has a solid security system. Even moderately skilled thieves are willing to spend only a limited amount of time gaining entrance, and they're likely to know just how much any given obstacle will slow them down.

Most security measures seek to achieve one of four primary goals:

- ▶ Make illegal entry harder

- ▶ Make illegal entry riskier

- ▶ Make illegal entry less rewarding

- ▶ Provide early warning of an illegal entry or attempted entry

Make it harder

As noted earlier, over 30% of unlawful entries are unforced. Open doors, unlocked doors, keys "hidden" under the doormat - all of these situations make it easy for an unskilled, opportunistic criminal to enter your home. Your goal is to make it hard enough to break in so that most burglars will either lack the skills or tools to enter, or will decide your home simply isn't worth the effort. There are always softer targets nearby.

Make it riskier

Criminals certainly don't want to get caught. Anything that increases the risk of apprehension is a deterrent to would-be intruders. A burglar alarm, for example – one that is monitored and armed – increases the chance that the intruder will be seen, heard, or confronted. A loud alarm siren can alert neighbors, and if a police unit happens to be nearby, even a rapid retreat might not prevent capture. The primary goals are often complementary, so "making it harder," also often adds "risk" due to the increased time required to enter. Most burglars aren't willing to spend more than a few minutes breaking into a home because the risk of being discovered or captured increases the longer they linger.

Make it less rewarding

A thief often knows what he or she intends to steal even before entering a home. Laptops, flat-screen televisions, electronics, jewelry, guns and cash are at the top of the list. You needn't throw out your valuables. Simply decreasing the expectation that such items will be in the home and unsecured can make your home seem a less rewarding target. Conversely, if you leave valuable property in plain view through an uncovered exterior window, you advertise the rewards that lie within your home. There is no benefit in offering criminals concrete incentives.

Provide early warning

Nothing is more important than your physical safety. If you are at home, a few seconds of warning that an illegal entry is in progress may offer time to call 9-1-1, to move your family to a safe room or perhaps even leave the premises. Alarm systems and motion activated lights are examples of measures that provide early warning. Doors and windows secured so thoroughly that thieves must break glass to gain entry also serve this purpose. Even if you are away from home and a burglary is in progress, an alarm system may warn you that it is unsafe to enter the home should you return.

The following checklists focus on security items in, around, and outside the home that help accomplish the four objectives: difficulty, risk, reward, and warning. Review these checklists against your own household and behavior. You'll have a clearer picture of steps you have taken – and steps you have not taken – to protect your home.

The Essential Home Security Checklist

Exterior Doors

The doors are locked: always when you are away (even for just a few minutes), as often as possible when at home, and always at night.	☐
All entry ways have a working, keyed entry lock and a high quality dead bolt lock installed into the frame of the door. The dead bolt throw is at least 1" in length, and the strike plate is secured to the wall studs -- not just the door frame -- with long screws	☐
Doors are made of solid, hardwood or metal.	☐
Door hinges cannot be removed from outside.	☐
Door frames are strong and fit tightly around the door. There is little or no gap that allows for easy prying.	☐
If door locks are within reach (40 inches) of windows, the window glass is either burglar resistant, shatterproof laminate, protected by burglar bars, or has been otherwise secured so that it cannot be broken to gain entry. Pet entrances or mail slots are not located in proximity to door locks.	☐
All exterior doors have a wide-angle (160-180 degree field of view) peephole installed at a height that all family members can use.	☐
Sliding glass doors have a working, keyed lock, not just a simple handle latch that can be easily defeated with a pry-bar.	☐

Sliding glass doors have either a "Charley bar," a strong dowel, or pins that prevent the door from being forced open. The door is always barred or pinned as well as locked when leaving home and at night.	☐
Sliding glass doors are adjusted, or use screws inside the top of the door frame, to prevent the door from being lifted from the tracks.	☐
Any doors from the garage or the basement that lead into the home are considered 'exterior doors' and have the same recommended security precautions for any other exterior door.	☐
Balcony or other second story, exterior doors are kept closed and locked when not in direct use. Second-story exterior doors have the same security precautions as first-floor exterior doors.	☐
Attic space entrances are securely locked with a hasp-lock and a pad-lock or an equally secure locking device.	☐
Keys to exterior doors or key rings that hold them do not contain a tag with personal information such as name, address, or any other data that could lead to your residence.	☐
Keys are not hidden under doormats, over the door, in mailboxes or elsewhere. An extra key has been given to a trusted neighbor or friend, or an extra key is kept locked up in an alternate location.	☐

The Essential Home Security Checklist

Windows

All windows in the home have working, keyed locks or pinning mechanisms that prevent the window from being easily opened if a glass pane is broken.	☐
Windows are either attended when open for ventilation or are opened no more than 6" and are locked or pinned in place to prevent them from being opened further.	☐
Windows that have single panes (large enough for a person to fit through without breaking window pane dividers or supports) have active, glass break or motion detectors, have burglar bars, or are made of shatterproof glass.	☐
Windows that are hidden, poorly lit, or otherwise offer an opportunity to enter the home are integrated into an alarm system or have security grills or screens or burglar bars in place.	☐
Where fire safety is a concern, emergency window exit needs are fully considered and appropriate measures to facilitate such exits are in place.	☐

Garages / Basements / Upstairs

Garage car doors are closed and locked unless the garage is in active use and occupied or attended.	☐

Garage car doors have a mechanical lock. The electric garage door opener is not relied upon as a security measure.	☐
Garage windows are covered or use treatments in such a way that the garage interior cannot be viewed from outside.	☐
Garage windows are secured shut with a locking sash or are pinned or nailed shut.	☐
Basement windows are kept closed and locked. Basement windows that do not need to be opened are tightly nailed shut.	☐
Second-story windows do not have untrimmed trees, branches or trellises (or unsecured ladders) nearby that allow easy access.	☐

Alarm Systems

A working, monitored alarm system is always set when leaving the house, even if only for a few minutes.	☐
The alarm system is always set at night.	☐
Entries and windows that can't be seen from the street or front of the residence are monitored by the alarm system. All bathroom windows or over-the-sink kitchen windows are monitored.	☐
Alarm company signs are clearly visible and indicate you have a security system.	☐

The Essential Home Security Checklist

Visibility and Lighting

The address or house number is clearly marked and illuminated so that police or fire department personnel can easily find your home should they respond to an alarm or a call.	☐
Bushes, shrubs, ground cover, and landscaping are kept well trimmed and do not offer a place for intruders to hide. There are no physical objects, such as large trash cans, that are placed in such a way as to offer a hiding place on your property.	☐
All exterior doors have a working light that clearly illuminates the area around the door and is switched from inside. Visitors to these doors can be clearly seen from inside the residence at night.	☐
Property floodlights are either left on at night or are motion activated. These lights cover all major areas of the property, leave no dark areas, nor do they create dark shadows around the home, garage, sheds or vegetation where a prowler could hide.	☐
Approaches to your property are well lit. Door lights are left on at night and when you are away from home, and a floodlight that is left on, or is activated by photo-cell or motion-sensor, illuminates the approach to your garage and yard gates.	☐
Shed or garage doors are illuminated at night or are covered by a motion activated light.	☐

The Appearance of Occupancy

A neighbor or friend collects mail, newspapers, and fliers when the home is unoccupied for more than a few days. A neighbor places the trash can at the collection point on the appropriate day.	☐
A second vehicle or a neighbor's vehicle is parked in front of the home or in the driveway when out of town.	☐
Arrangements to have the lawn mowed are made if you are away for a week or more.	☐
Arrangements to have snow shoveled from sidewalks are made whenever you are away from home.	☐
At least two interior lights are on automatic timers programmed to turn on and off at irregular intervals when you are away from home. At least one light is on at all times, and one timed light is located in a bathroom. Timers and/or lamps are located so that a thief cannot see that an automatic device is in use.	☐
Your telephone answering service message does not say whether you are home, out of the home, or on vacation and it does not reveal your full name.	☐
Telephone ringers are turned down or off when you are on vacation.	☐
Shades, drapes and blinds are closed in a majority of rooms when you are away, but the house is not overtly closed-up and unoccupied. Enough of the home is obscured that it is difficult for a potential intruder to determine by looking into windows that the home is unoccupied.	☐

The Essential Home Security Checklist

Protecting Valuables

Important documents and valuables are kept in a safety deposit box or, at minimum, in a locked home safe.	☐
Home safes are secured to flooring, wall studs or other solid structures with bolts that can only be accessed when the safe is open. Home safes are *not* anchored to drywall or other less-than sturdy material.	☐
Property has been photographed or videotaped, serial numbers have been recorded, and these records are kept at a separate location from the residence.	☐
Where possible, property has been marked with an electric engraver, or with security-grade, waterproof invisible ink.	☐

Object Visibility

Shades, drapes or blinds obscure enough of the home so that it is difficult for a potential intruder to visually determine if the home is occupied. Blinds or shades for offices, media rooms, or other rooms with numerous theft-targeted items are always kept closed when not occupied.	☐
Laptops, cameras and other items at high risk for theft are not left out in the open. They are kept in cupboards or closets or otherwise out of sight when not in use.	☐

Outdoors

Lawn mowers, portable gas grills, snow blowers and other valuable equipment are locked in the garage or in a storage shed. If items must be left in the open, they are covered with a tarp, out of plain view and chain-locked to a secure structure.	☐
Bicycles that are unattended, no matter how briefly, are always locked to a fixed structure with a quality chain lock or bicycle lock.	☐
Tools and ladders are kept locked indoors or in the garage.	☐
You do not use your full name on your mailbox.	☐
Exterior sheds and gates are locked with laminated, high-security pad-locks with a shrouded shackle design.	☐

Digital Essentials

You never announce travel plans on social media or post photographs or updates of your vacation when travelling.	☐
You do not use an e-mail auto-response that indicates you are out of town or away from home.	☐
You don't post photographs or updates of your vacation when travelling to any picture sharing or social site. Wait until you've returned home.	☐
You don't rely on privacy settings to protect information you post on or send through social media sites.	☐

CHAPTER 4
Enacting The Checklists

If you took an honest self-inventory using the checklists in chapter three, you likely identified items that you can correct.   While all of the items on the list can improve your security situation, don't be concerned if your personal budget or other issues prevent you from taking each and every action, and don't feel overwhelmed if you've discovered many problem areas. Very few can check even half the boxes on the checklists. The key is to take action, tackling one problem at a time.

Prioritizing Security Measures

Determine your most vulnerable areas and those that concern you the most. Perhaps you worry about a side window that doesn't properly latch or lock. Perhaps you dislike coming home at night because your property is dark. Fix these problems, then re-evaluate to determine the next-weakest security point. Understand that you cannot eliminate weaknesses. However, knowing where thieves tend to look for easy access gives you an advantage. If doors are extremely secure, a thief will likely look to windows, or vice-versa. If a window is pry resistant, the thief may break the window glass.   A thief may well give up when thwarted by locked, pinned, or otherwise secure windows or by windows too small for entry even with the glass broken. Prioritize and address weakest areas first and remember that your primary goal is to make it harder, riskier and less rewarding to break into your home.

Maintaining Perspective

Robert Frost wrote in his poem, Mending Wall, "Something there is that doesn't love a wall." He spoke of endlessly frustrating efforts to maintain a stone wall continually breached by nature and by man. Like Frost's wall, no home is impenetrable, and you could work endlessly to shore up the weakest link – only to find that doing so exposes a new weak link.

The purpose of this book is not to turn you into a paranoid and frightened home-security zealot. On the contrary, the book offers you a series of measures that allow you to sleep better at night and relax when you are away from home. Again, focus on enacting the measures you identify as high-priority. You will find that once you take control and action with regard to security, greater peace of mind often follows.

If you have recently been a crime victim, you may feel a need to take significant action, a need driven by fear, anger, or a need to regain some feeling of control. Taking concrete security action may help, but reaction to trauma varies from person to person. If your emotions don't subside with time, talk to a counselor or therapist, as no one should have to live in constant fear

Focus

There is no need to read all of the following sections through and through, although you may learn something in doing so. It is important to direct your efforts towards the areas that both require attention and that you can improve. Feel free to skip topics you "passed" on the checklist or that otherwise do not apply to you. Focus first on measures you can and will take in the near future

When to Ask for Help

Finally, if for any reason you feel you can't properly assess your safety and security, or if you are not comfortable replacing or installing any of the recommend hardware or measures, contact a qualified locksmith, security professional, or a trusted and knowledgeable friend or handyman for assistance.

CHAPTER 5
Exterior Doors

Door Construction and Material

Most standard exterior home doors used by building contractors are low cost units. A strong intruder can kick a typical exterior door down with stunning speed, and this method of illegal entry is all too common. You, or the professionals or friends you have chosen to assist you, must first determine if entry doors need repair or replacement. Use the following guidelines.

▶ Are they metal, solid hardwood or hollow core? Do not use hollow core doors, or any door originally designed for interior use, as an exterior door. If you have a hollow exterior door, don't waste money upgrading the locks. Replace the door with a solid wood or metal door.

▶ Are the doors *and* door frames in good condition and free of rot? Do doors fit tightly and securely in the frames, or have they sagged or shifted, leaving gaps that allow easy insertion of prying tools?

▶ Will doors, locks and frames withstand repeated kicking?

▶ Are there windows nearby (within about 40 inches) that, if broken, allow someone to reach in and open the door locks?

If you have exterior doors with any of these weaknesses, repair or replace them with solid wood or steel doors that have no windows or that have simple skylight windows out of reach of the door lock. A steel door, properly installed, will be very strong as

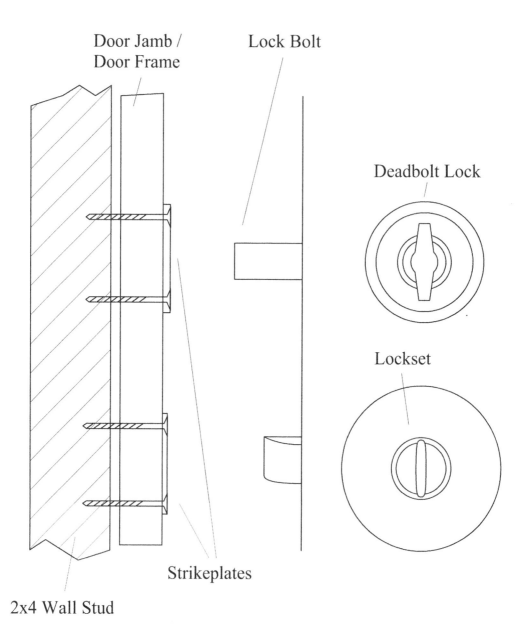

Door Jamb /
Door Frame

Lock Bolt

Deadbolt Lock

Lockset

Strikeplates

2x4 Wall Stud

Door locks and the structures that support them. Strong door frames, high-quality, extra-long lock bolts and well-secured strike plates all help locks resists force applied to the door or lock.

long as the door frames are in good condition and the door is equipped with quality locks. Inspect the inside doorjamb (the vertical sides of the door frame) material for rot and cracking. Many hardware stores, most locksmiths, and a host of security vendors offer steel reinforcement plates -- or even entire door frame liners for serious prying resistance -- that may be added to strengthen existing door frames. Reinforcements are only as strong as the material they're anchored to and should feature screws that extend well into structural studs.

Exterior Door Locks

If your exterior doors do not have high quality, dead-bolt locks, consider this a priority. A dead bolt is a lock that retracts or opens only when the lock cylinder is rotated. Dead bolts (unlike spring locks commonly built into door handles) cannot be retracted by simply applying force to the bolt. Install a Grade 1 (look for the letters "ANSI" next to the grade) hardened steel, dead bolt lock with a bolt that extends at least 1" into the strike plate and door frame. Longer bolts are better, as length

makes it more difficult to pry or spread the door frame enough to free the bolt from the strike plate. If your home currently has a dead bolt, don't assume that you have a *quality* dead bolt. Most building codes don't specify lock quality, and in some cases don't even mandate a lock. If you currently have a dead bolt lock on an exterior door that doesn't meet the above criteria, replace it. For older locks, gauge the lock condition by testing the key. A good dead-bolt lock should have very little play and have a smooth but solid feel when the key is turned. If there is a lot of play in the mechanics, it's

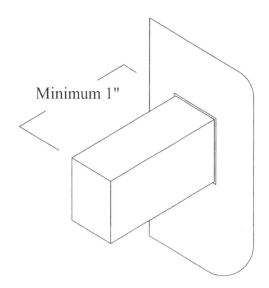

Minimum 1"

Lock bolts should be at least 1" long

likely there is enough internal wear to warrant replacement.

Additional features to look for in a dead-bolt lock:

▶ Saw-resistant bolts, in which an internal pin rolls with the motion of a saw, make sawing off the bolt extremely difficult

▶ Some anti-drill locks feature hardened steel chips embedded in the lock casing. If the thief attempts to "drill out" a lock, this feature will simply ruin most drill bits.

▶ Key control is available from some manufacturers. Key control means that keys cannot be copied by generic hardware store key machines or kiosks but must be copied at a locksmith authorized by the lock maker.

Alternatively, surface mounted dead bolts are quick to install, and can be effective provided both the lock and lock bolt receiver are very securely fastened to the door and to the door frame.

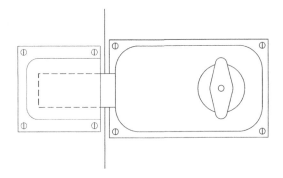

Surface mounted deadbolts install without cutting a hole through the door

If for some reason a dead bolt is not an option, get the highest quality entry lock set you can afford. Ask your locksmith or hardware store to advise you for your particular application. If using a lock set instead of a dead bolt, be absolutely certain that the lock has an automatic dead-latch feature. This prevents the bolt from compressing back into the lock. Without a dead-latch feature, a thief using a credit card or even a table knife can slip the bolt open.

Remember, too, that unforced entry is common. A lock is no help if intruders have a key or if you unlock it for them. The following list may seem elementary, or some of the items may appear extreme. Yet for the frail, the elderly, or for children, some of the most obvious and cautious guidelines are worthy and merit review.

▶ Always re-key door locks if you move into a new residence or if you lose your keys. Give keys or access to keys to household help only when necessary, and re-key if the help leaves your employment.

▶ Criminals routinely pose as repair people, technicians, salespeople, or others who might have a legitimate reason to approach the home. The old advice that says "don't open the door for unexpected strangers no matter how innocent they may appear," always applies.

▶ Ask scheduled service or repair personnel for picture I.D., and never admit unscheduled personnel into your home.

▶ Keep an eye on service personnel while they are in your home, and check *all* window and door locks -- particularly bathroom window latches -- after they leave.

▶ If a package is delivered or someone wishes to give you something, ask the deliverer to place the item on the porch or landing and to leave the premises.

▶ If you must sign for a delivery, have the document slipped to you under the door or through a mail slot.

▶ Don't open the doors or exit the house unless you are certain any strangers have departed the premises and the area.

Double-Cylinder Dead Bolts: Special Considerations

Double-cylinder dead bolts are locks that require a key *both inside and outside* the home to lock and unlock. This prevents thieves from manually unlocking doors through a broken window or a mail slot, but carries distinct safety considerations. First, if you're considering a double-cylinder dead bolt, you should check with your local codes, as double-cylinder dead bolts may be prohibited where you live, usually due to fire-code restrictions. Second, avoid double-cylinder dead bolts on any door that might need to serve as a primary fire escape. If you need to make a rapid exit out this door, it may be difficult if the key is not handy. You can leave the key near the door but out of sight to allow for emergency exit. However, should you need to exit quickly, you'll have to pick up the key (assuming it's been left in its proper place) and insert it in the lock. Your hands may not be particularly steady if you're threatened by fire or are retreating from an intruder already in the home.

Another option is to leave the key in the lock when you are home so that anyone that needs to get out can do so quickly. Note that as long as a key is in the lock, it is no more secure than a thumb-turned dead bolt.

One key solution borrows a technique from scuba diving. To safeguard against gear loss, divers use retractors, small, durable devices that spool out strong, nylon line. These devices usually contain a clip of some sort on the retractor housing and another clip on the end of the line. A spring reels in the line. One security-conscious diver installed a double-cylinder dead bolt in his home. He attached a scuba style retractor to the wall a little over three feet from the entrance door, out of reach and out of sight from nearby windows. He attached a spare door key to the retractor line, insuring that the key was always in a consistent spot and in reasonable proximity to the lock. Misplacing or dropping the key was not at issue as the retractor simply reeled it back into place on the wall when not in use. Retractors aren't exclusively used in diving and are sold at most hardware stores if this solution interests you.

You should carefully weight the drawbacks to double-cylinder locks against the security advantages. If you do opt for such a lock, have a system in place for how you and your family will handle keys and emergency exits.

Strike Plate Security

To secure a strike plate (the hardware that receives the lock bolt), replace the standard short screws with three to four-inch screws that drive completely through the door frame and into the studs surrounding the frame. Use three or four screws instead of the standard two whenever possible. The strike plate is often the weakest link in door security. If the door is kicked, the force concentrates against the points holding the door in place: the hinges, the lock bolt, and the strike plate that keeps the lock bolt in place. Even the highest quality lock loaded with features is of little help if the strike plate easily breaks away from the door frame.

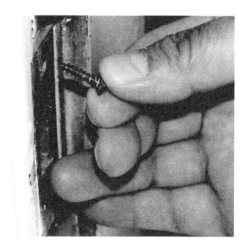

Typical strike plate screws are too short. Use 3-inch screws (or longer) to secure the strike-plate to the wall stud

Hinges

Most exterior doors have hinge mechanisms on the inside face of the door. If you have an exterior door with hinge pins on the outside of the door, the best solution replaces any door with interior hinges or reinstalls the door so that the hinge pins are inside. Otherwise, a burglar only needs to remove the hinge pins and lift the door from the frame, regardless of the quality of your locks.

However, some areas prone to civil emergencies such as hurricanes have building codes that require exterior door hinges. If you live in such an area, you'll need to use another method to secure the hinges. It's possible to weld the hinge pins in place, but this makes it difficult if the door ever needs servicing, and codes in your area may prohibit that solution.

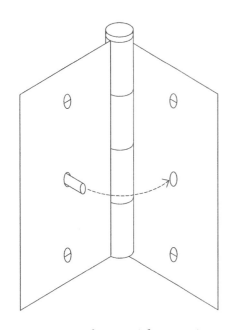

To secure a door with exterior hinge pins, replace an opposing set of hinge screws with a headless nail or short metal rod.

Another method is to remove two opposite-facing screws from the hinge facing (see diagram). Insert a strong nail snugly into the wall side. Cut the nail length so that, when the door closes, it forms a simple "dead bolt" through both hinge faces. Even if the hinge pins are removed, the door can't easily be lifted out of place.

There are hinge screws on the market designed just for this purpose. These screws have narrow heads enabling them to work like a nail in this solution, but are more securely anchored. Be sure to contact a security company or your local police bureau for advice on what is allowed and recommended in your area.

Adjacent Windows

If your exterior door has windows or a sidelight within 3 ½ feet of the door locks, a hand-turned dead-bolt lock will be easy to defeat. The thief need only break the window and reach in to open the lock. If door replacement or security glass are beyond your means, consider installing a second dead bolt lock too far to reach through any nearby broken window. Be sure to positioned any secondary dead bolt at least six inches from the bottom or top of the door. If the central dead bolt has been opened via a window, a secondary lock located too close to the top or bottom of the door will allow the door to twist in the door frame under force. Still, any sec-

ondary dead bolt that cannot be reached through a window or mail slot may buy you some warning, as it will be harder for a thief to enter quietly. Alternatively, replace the window glass (or glazing) with security or bulletproof glass or install a metal security grid. Security glass is usually not glass at all, but a synthetic resin that is highly resistant to breakage. Security-reinforcing films also are on the market that apply to the existing glass. All but very high quality reinforcing films are unlikely to stop an intruder determined to break the glass. Any film that withstands several blows, though, may give you additional warning time if you are in the home.

Although equipped with a dead bolt lock, this door is not secure. Either the adjacent window or the in-door windows allow a thief to reach the lock if the glass is broken

Peepholes

If you have a solid door, install a peephole (a small viewing lens inserted through your door) with the widest-angle view of you can find -- a 180 degree view is best. Position the lens slightly under five feet from the bottom of the door. This height works even for a youngster if a step stool is nearby, and ensures a good view of those outside. Peephole lenses are available at your local hardware store and installation requires little more than a drill and a wrench. Most handymen can install such a lens for you. The high-tech version of peepholes, video "doorbells" are on the market for $200-$300. These systems use battery powered or hard-wired cameras and small viewing screens to allow those inside the home to see who is at the door. Some video doorbells incorporate intercom systems, electronic locking systems and other features. Unless you're motivated to spend the extra money or seek specific features, a standard peephole will serve the purpose and won't be subject to battery or circuit failure.

Portable Door Braces

Several companies manufacture door braces or "jammers" that can help brace doors against forced entry. These are adjustable-length poles with a "U" shaped or slotted end designed to hook under the doorknob and a rubber (or similar) footing to brace against the floor. Like dead bolts, if the brace release feature can be reached through a window, mail slot or pet door, they are useless. However, these devices can provide quick, temporary security in hotel rooms and other housing. Doorknob alarms that sound if the knob is turned may also be useful in motels or hotels.

Sliding Glass Doors - Issues and Solutions

Architectural trends dating back to 1950 favor sliding glass doors, also known as patio doors or Arcadia doors after a well known manufacturer. Although they admit much light and have an open feel, they present unique security concerns. Primarily, the "locks" on most sliding doors are little more than a short, hook latch that easily pries open.

A simple wooden rod placed into sliding glass door tracks makes forced door opening difficult.

A locksmith can upgrade your existing latch with a higher quality security latch, in most cases one that requires key access from the outside. Your locksmith will also likely recommend a latch guard, a simple metal shield that makes inserting prying tools near the lock mechanism difficult. The least expensive patio door security measure is a 1" thick wooden dowel or bar inserted into the lower track –

one that is long enough to allow the door to open no more than a few inches.

"Charley bars" are an enhanced variation of a simple dowel doorstop, and are not difficult to install. A Charley bar consists of a metal bar or tube that mounts between the wall or door frame and the sliding section of the door. These bars are hinged, allowing users to lift and secure them out of the way or to lower them into a catch mechanism that prevents the door from opening. A well-made Charley bar will be as secure but more convenient than a simple dowel, especially for the elderly, as they do not require bending or kneeling if they are mounted mid-way up the door frame.

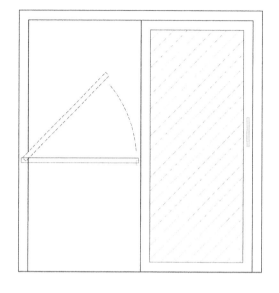

Charley bars work much like a dowel, but mount to the door frame. A hinge permits folding out of the way when not in use

Finally, many sliding glass doors permit "lifting" from the sliding tracks, even if a bar is in place. If your door is not equipped with a sturdy adjustment mechanism to prevent this, you may insert several (preferably three) 1" to 1 1/2" screws into the door's upper track recess. Space screws about a foot apart, and adjust them until the top of the door does not hit or scrape the screw heads but minimally clears them when closed. This allows the

Sliding glass doors can't be lifted from the frame if screws in the upper track are adjusted to block upward movement of the sliding door frame

door to open freely but the screws will block lifting the door from the tracks.

Several manufacturers offer pre-made pins that 'lock' many makes of sliding glass doors. These pins place into aligned holes (with door in closed position) drilled both through the fixed frame and the sliding frame. The door won't slide open unless the in-place pin is sheared or broken. Most, but not all door frame designs accommodate pins, so be certain you will not damage your door glass before you begin to drill. Ask a security or qualified handyman for assistance if you are uncertain. For convenience, secure the bolt or pin to a chain or line attached to the door or adjacent wall so it won't be misplaced.

Hidden Keys

It's astoundingly common practice to hide a spare key under a doormat, above the door, or in another "clever" place. Don't. Thieves can and will find them. If you simply must have a spare key on the exterior property, an industrial quality key lockbox, such as those used by realtors, is an option. It's best if the lock box is well out of sight, and it must be securely mounted to studs or sturdy, structural material. Still, these boxes won't hold up against a heavy hammer or other tools. The best option is to give a backup key to a trusted neighbor or friend.

Second Story Doors

Most upper-story doors lead out onto a patio or a deck. The chances of a break-in on an upper floor are less than on the ground floor. This does not justify foregoing security measures on upper floors, particularly given that many second story doors are sliding-glass doors. Secure all second story, sliding glass doors with a pin, dowel or Charley bar. (See sliding glass doors). Whenever possible, apply security to second story doors just as you would to ground floor entry doors.

Step outside and visually assess the difficulty of accessing your second-story patio or deck. If you have a staircase leading from the ground to, say, a deck, there's not much you can do about access, and highlights the need for other measures. Assuming there are no stairs, take a look at other ways an intruder might reach the balcony. Are there tree branches close enough to the patio that would allow some-one to reach it by climbing? Don't underestimate the athletic abilities of intruders. Trim branches well back from any second story patios or doors and windows. If there are trellises or other structures that would aid access, move or remove them. Make it as hard as possible to reach the second-story entrance without a ladder.

Chain Locks and Bar Guards

In one recent crime report, a man knocked at a home and claimed to be looking for a lost dog. To accept a flyer on the missing animal, the home's occupant, a single woman, cautiously opened the door with the chain lock in place. The intruder easily snapped the chain mechanism with a single kick and beat and robbed the woman. Standard chain locks rarely offer any real protection against a strong door kick. Some swinging bars, as often seen in hotels, are sturdier in construc-tion than chains, but require very secure anchoring. It's not worth putting any of these devices to a real-world test by opening a door unnecessarily. Use a peephole instead. Remember: The door is strongest when closed in the door frame and with bolts locked.

Securing Garage, Basement, and Attic Entries

Treat doors that enter your home from the garage or basement (garage vehicle doors are covered in the section devoted to garages) just like other exterior entry doors. Basements and garages are often targets for entry as they are less likely to be occupied - and doors from the basement or garage into the house are less likely to be locked securely. The thief may enter your basement or garage, wait in hiding until certain the home is empty or, worse, enter the home with the knowledge that you are there. For this reason, door construction, locks and all other items sug-gested for an exterior door should be in place -- and in use -- for garage and basement home entries.

Although not common, intruders have used attics to gain entry into homes. Use solid keyed locks, or hasps with strong padlocks on any attic doors, pull-down staircases, or crawl-space entrances.

CHAPTER 6
Windows

Windows present numerous security challenges. Not only is glass particularly vulnerable, but windows vary enormously in style, material and construction. Window security focuses on three primary goals: prevent the window from being opened wide enough to permit entry, prevent breaking or removal of window glass, and provide a warning if either event occurs.

Windows contain three elements, the glass (or glazing), the sash and the full window frame. The window glass mounts into the sash, which may be moveable/sliding or fixed and is usually aluminum, steel, wood or vinyl. The sashes mount into the window frame, which occupies the rough wall opening.

Window Types

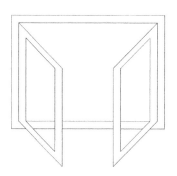

▶ Casement windows swing open on hinges like a door. Some casement windows open with a crank mechanism. Windows may be single sash or double sash design.   Sometimes referred to as "French" windows due to the design similarity.

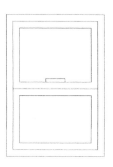

▶ Vertical sliding windows, single or double-hung and usually constructed of wood, metal, or vinyl, are common.   "Single hung" means only one of the sashes may be opened, while both sashes slide if a window is "double hung." These windows often contain a single pane of glass per sash. One or two "crescent" fasteners generally secure the window when closed. These fasteners, unless locked in place with a key, are easy to defeat.

▶ Horizontal sliding windows work much like a sliding glass doors and have similar considerations. The sashes are susceptible to prying or, particularly with older models, lifting from the window track.

▶ Jalousie, or louvered windows, consist of a series of horizontal panes of glass that close and open mechanically. These are most common in older homes in southern, coastal regions.

▶ Awnings are windows hinged at either top or bottom, and rotate inward or outward when opened. Awning-type openings are in common use as basement windows in older homes.

▶ Fixed windows contain no hinges or mechanism for opening.

▶ Sashless windows are uncommon and generally have counter-balanced glass panes. The glazing/glass does not sit within a sash frame. These windows are typically custom built, and usually have built-in security features. If you have such a window and it lacks strong locks or security measures, consult a locksmith to review your options.

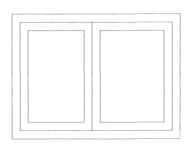 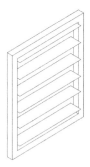 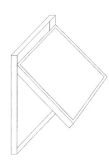

Horizontal Sliding   *Jalousie Window*   *Awning*

Securing Windows

Alarm Monitoring Benefits and Limitations

If you have an alarm system, integrating windows into the system is important to deter thieves or, at minimum, provide a warning to you in the event a burglar opens a window. Sensor designs allow incorporation of almost any window type into your alarm system. There are even window screens that double as alarm sensors. These screens lock to the window frame so securely that an intruder will usually choose to quickly cut the screen. Cutting breaks small sensor wires within the screen mesh and triggers an alarm.   Although screen sensors are more expensive than a simple window alarm sensor, thieves may be frightened away before glass is broken or window frames damaged by prying tools.

Windows with multiple, french-door style panes offer entry via breaking (or some-times quietly prying out) a single, small pane of glass. The thief may then reach in, unfasten the window lock, and open the window. Although opening a monitored window will trigger an alarm, the intruder may instantly enter the home. To minimize this problem, use keyed sash locks, push locks, or pin locks, or any locking device that can't be easily unfastened with bare hands.

Thieves that breaks glass only to find that window locks still prevent a rapid entry may move on, concerned that even more measures are in place. These locking devices do secure the sashes on large, single or double-paned windows. However, a very large pane of glass, once broken, may simply allow a thief to climb in *through* the sash. A little broken glass won't slow them down for more than a second or two. Strongly consider using glass-break alarms if you have large-paned windows, par-ticularly if you have such windows on the ground floor. For more details on window alarm sensors and options, see Chapter 8: Burglar Alarms. *Remember that secur-ing windows against entry may also hinder exit.* Read all the information on window fire safety information in this chapter and consider the emergency exit needs of your residence carefully.

Keyed Sash Locks

Keyed sash locks replace your existing window fasteners. Your can fit your entire house with sash locks that open with one key. Keyed windows require that you

consider the possible need to exit through a window quickly, perhaps in the event of fire. To permit easy escape, keep keys handy (but out of plain sight) near all keyed windows. Ensure that family members know where keys are for all windows that might serve as a necessary escape.

Pinning Windows

Pin or bolt window locks operate much like a dead bolt lock on a door. A lock mechanism with a sliding bolt or a pin fastens to the either the window sash or window frame, depending on the window design. The lock bolt slides into a receiver (it works much like a strike plate) or, sometimes, simply into a hole drilled in the window frame or sash. The lock place-ment and receiver are aligned so that the lock may be engaged when the window is closed. Keyed pin-lock models are available and may be useful if sash locks aren't practical for your window style. You may drill several bolt holes or install several receivers for use with a single pin lock: one that permits locking in closed position, another that permits locking the window ajar for ventilation. The ventilated position should lock the window open no more than five inches.

You can also "pin" a window without a dedicated locking product by drilling a hole (or holes) at downward angles through the sash and into the window frame or through both sashes if double hung (see illustration on page 50). Insert strong nails, 8 gauge or thicker, into these holes to "pin" windows in place. Be certain the nail is long enough to fully engage the sash and the frame or both sashes. Trim the length of the nail if necessary so that the head lies flush against the frame when fully engaged. Though removable by hand, the nail won't be readily noticeable. This type of pinning makes it hard to quickly open the

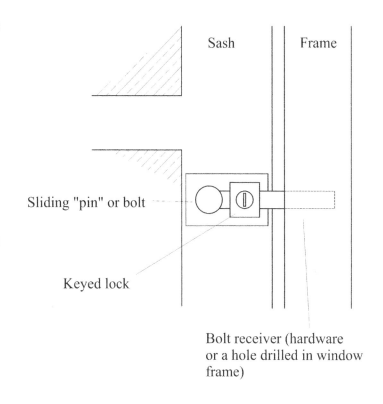

A basic window "pin" or bolt lock. This sample is keyed. Engaging the bolt or pin secures the sash and frame together; the window cannot be opened.

window without breaking glass. Even if an intruder breaks the glass, locating and removing the nails or pins will delay entry. To make a thief's job tougher, cut the heads off the nails completely, but if you do, keep a strong magnet nearby to remove the nails (and never use copper of aluminum nails). As with pin locks, drill holes for both closed and ventilated positions as desired. Note that if a thief tries to pry a nail pinned window, the nails may bend and the window may lock up. The nails can be very difficult to remove if this happens, particularly if you've opted to cut off the nail heads. Inexpensive, aluminum windows may not offer easy or secure sash-to-frame nail pinning options. Most aluminum windows slide in a track that is attached to the window frame, as opposed to a groove in the frame. You can drill a hole through

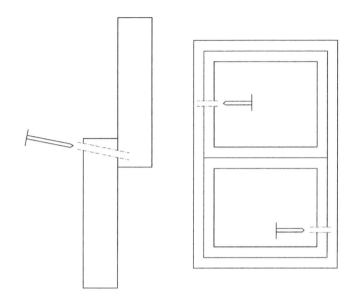

Many window designs accommodate pinning with a nail or bolt. Pin two sashes together (above left) or pin sashes to the window frame (above right)

A bolt secured in the guide frame of this aluminum window prevents opening more than a few inches

the track just above or next to the window sash. Place a strong bolt through the hole and tighten it with a standard or wing nut. The top of the window sash will hit the bolt if someone tries to open it. Use non-standard bolts that require more than a screwdriver or a wrench. A bolt-head that only accepts an Allen wrench (a driver or wrench with a hexagon shaped head) is a good choice.

Amateur or impromptu thieves aren't likely to carry a full set of Allen wrenches. If the window design permits, even a bolt cutter may not work if bolts are in a hard-to-reach position within the window track. Although these -- or any -- methods are not foolproof, they'll slow a thief down, require that they break glass, and discourage intruders lacking the appropriate tools. One method to facilitate emergency escape leaves a bolt in place, but unsecured by a nut, on at least one designated window in each room.

Screw-Down and Friction Locks

Perhaps your window construction won't accommodate sash-locks or pinning, or you rent and can't drill holes in your window frames. There are alternative window locking products on the market. Common, screw-down window locks, which use the friction of a hand-tightened screw against the window track, prevent horizontal or vertical windows from sliding open without force. Thumbscrew locks can prevent a window from being easily jim-mied. However, they must be tightened with force, and can be quickly removed if a glass pane is broken. It's best to use friction screw locks that have a unique head (several models offer unique, triangular designs) that requires a special tool or key to turn. While screw down devices can be effective against some intrusion efforts, the best ways to secure window sashes are keyed, locking window fasteners (sash locks), or pins or other mechanisms that physically couple the window sash and frame together.

Thumbscrew friction locks must be tight-ened down hard to prevent prying open the window

Mechanical Casement Cranks

Casement windows are most secure if they open via a mechanical crank, as this design usually demands that the glass be broken to gain entry. If you have case-ment windows that open freely, consider installing a crank or lever opening mecha-nism. In addition, install one of the many keyed lock types available for this window style.

Jalousie Windows

Jalousie or louvered windows are extremely difficult to secure via locks or pins alone. The very best solution for jalousie windows, besides replacing them, is to professionally install a strong security screen or grate.

Glass Security

In the early morning hours in a southern city, a newly married couple recently wakened to find a large man standing in their bedroom. Although the intruder fled when he encountered an unexpected male in the home, the couple felt particularly shocked, as they had set their functioning, home alarm system before they went to bed. Police found that the thief had cut the glass in a picture window and created an opening large enough to crawl through. The intruder entered via a window with an active alarm sensor *without triggering the alarm*. It's not comforting to know that some offenders such as rapists seek homes that are occupied. They may cut or otherwise remove large glass panes to gain silent entry into the home, or they may apply tape to windows before breaking to reduce noise. Sash locks, pins, and other devices that prevent the window from opening -- and the alarm system -- are all bypassed. If you have ground floor windows featuring sizeable, single panes of glass, employ extra measures to prevent such an entry.

There are several alarm sensor types that warn of window glass tampering. Inexpensive motion or vibration detector alarms attach to glass panes and trigger in the event of unusual motion, and these may offer some warning, but do not prevent entry. Note that thunderstorms or other loud noises may also trigger motion sensor alarms. If you are interested in protecting windows with a more concrete deterrent than an alarm, consider replacing the glazing with tempered glass (it's difficult to cut.), or with security or "bullet proof" glass. Security films, as mentioned for use in windows proximate to door locks, are also an option. These films vary greatly in thickness, quality and durability. The best products are surprisingly tough, and offer enough breakage resistance to cause many thieves to simply give up.

Security Screens and Burglar Bars

Once viewed as a measure of last resort, burglar bars, often marketed as security screens or grates, are a reasonably affordable, extremely secure method of protecting windows. Many homeowners dislike screens, grates, or bars because they may imply (based on reasonable and historical perception) that a neighborhood is not safe -- and thereby diminish property values. Today, improved designs that blend in with or accent the architecture are widely on the market. These "designer burglar bars" are increasingly used in high end homes and neighborhoods. Few thieves will tackle the challenge of defeating a locked security grate or burglar bar, stylish or not, unless they have special equipment or skills or they believe there is extremely valuable property beyond.

Burglar bars, screens or grates install either on the interior or exterior of the window based on design. If there is any possibility that a window may serve as a fire escape, do not install rigid and fixed window bars. Use only hinged or collapsible screens or bars that can be unlocked and opened in an emergency. Keep

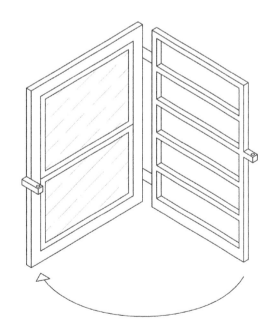

Burglar bars offer strong security, although home owners may consider some designs unattractive

keys in a consistent, convenient place and make sure all family members know how to open the screen or bars in an emergency. Many firefighters rightfully regard fixed security bars as a hazard, as many designs will resist even heavy blows from a fireman's ax *from the interior of the home*. Firefighters have lost their lives when fixed security bars prevented exit from a burning structure.

More on Windows and Fire Security

Most window security measures work both ways: they hinder both rapid entry and exit. It's critical to consider fire safety or other emergency exit needs as you secure windows from intruders. Make sure family members have quick access to any keys, and know how to unlock windows or remove pins. If you secure windows with bolts or screws, define specific fire exit windows and ensure escape is quick and easy. In a bedroom with multiple windows, for example, select the window that offers the fastest escape route and make sure any security devices unfasten, preferably without tools, for quick removal and escape. All family members should be aware of fire escape routes and fire escape windows. If a window opens with notable difficulty, be sure family members understand that, in the event of an emergency, it will be necessary to throw a piece of furniture or other large object completely through the window to allow rapid escape. Unless their lives are in imminent danger, they should first clear away glass shards with a hard object and place a blanket or other material into the window frame to help guard against cuts as they exit. You may need special precautions for children, the elderly, or disabled individuals.

Basement, Garage and Second Story Windows

Horror movies frequently feature basement scenes for good reason. Subterranean settings are often dark, and house plumbing pipes, water heaters, furnaces, duct work or other fixtures that create deep shadows and offer excellent hiding places. Prying or breaking low-to-the ground basement windows reduces the chance of alerting someone within the home unless the basement is occupied. Burglar bars or a security grates are often an effective solution if they do not violate local codes or otherwise create a fire safety concern. The "bad neighborhood" stigma that may accompany burglar bars usually isn't an issue with basement windows as they tend to be out of sight from the street. If your basement is not used as a living space, your local codes may allow you to nail basement windows shut. Otherwise, use locking or monitoring methods similar to those you apply on ground floor windows.

Garage windows that offer easy entry are most common in older homes. Garage windows rarely have curtains or shades, so intruders can often see if anyone is in the garage. Cover windows or use opaque treatments. Install keyed locks on garage windows (or nail them shut if they're never used) and install window-vibration sensors with a loud alarm or siren. Whether you connect these sensors to your primary alarm system or not, a loud alarm may make enough noise to cause a thief to flee. Still, a bold or aggressive thief may understand that a garage alarm may not be audible to those inside the house. They may ignore the alarm and attempt to enter the home, emphasizing the essential need to treat garage entrances as exterior doors.

Second story windows are a far less likely entry point than ground floor windows, but this is no reason to leave them unsecured. Keyed sash locks and/or pins force an intruder to spend time perched on a ladder while fiddling with tools or pry bars, a less than ideal situation for anyone wishing to avoid detection and maintain the ability to flee quickly. As with second story doors, make sure there are no tree limbs or a scalable trellis nearby. A large branch growing next to a window might offer an intruder both easy access and concealment.

CHAPTER 7
Garage and Yard

If you have an attached garage, it is likely the least secure entry into your home. The garage offers a measure of privacy and may give an intruder plenty of time – and in many cases a nice set of tools. If a thief is able to enter your garage through a window or carport entrance, they may have everything they need to defeat an otherwise secure door leading into the household. Secure exterior entrances into the garage just as you secure entries into the home.

Garage Locks

Don't rely on your standard, electric garage door opener as a "lock." Instead, use a sliding garage door lock or cylinder handle lock. Either of these sell at minimal cost and fit almost any garage door configuration. Locks that secure car entrances are available with features designed for both detached garages and attached garages (the latter may have an additional, interior-only lock). These locks do require that you exit the car and add inconvenience in exchange for garage security. At the very least, secure these locks when you are at home, particularly if your garage is attached and offers direct entry into the home.

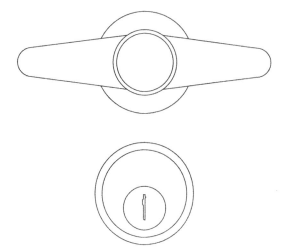

While less convenient than relying on your automatic garage door opener, a keyed garage door lock, such as this cylinder handle lock, offers greater security.

Garage Remote Controls

Garage door remote openers, particularly older models, are often not as secure as you might think. Garage door remote controls that use a static code are susceptible to a practice known as code grabbing. Thieves intercept the wireless signal and the code transmitted by the garage remote and store it. Once you're away from home, they simply retransmit the code and easily open your garage. No particular technical sophistication is required of the thief, and code grabbing devices are not difficult to obtain.

Protect yourself from this threat with a rolling-code remote. Rolling code systems randomly change the code with each use. Many of these devices have millions or billions of potential combinations. Thieves can still capture codes, but they won't work. The cost to convert remote systems that use a single code to a rolling or multiple code systems costs around $50.

Don't forget less technical threats. Never leave a garage remote attached to the visor of your vehicle or in any other spot that is in plain view. While many people routinely keep their remote controls on car visors, in practice this is akin to leaving your house keys dangling from your rear-view mirror. It's simply not sensible.

Garage Alarms

Attached garages are a common entry point for thieves, so it's wise to include all garage doors and windows in your alarm system. Fortunately, many sensor types are now available as wireless devices, so the need for hard wiring (and the subsequent cost) isn't as great as it was just a few years ago. Three or four sensors will, in most cases, cover all doors and windows in a typical two-car garage.

If you don't have a central alarm system, or if your existing alarm system won't accommodate additional sensors, an inexpensive supplemental system is much better than no system at all. Install readily available, magnetic, battery operated, "open or shut" door alarms on exterior-to-garage doors and on garage windows. Many of these tiny devices sound sirens so loud they hurt the ears if you're close by. Consider these more as a deterrent to thieves than as an early warning to you. These alarms may be surprisingly loud for their size, but you still may not hear them if you are inside and on the far side of the house. However, a thief won't immediately know whether you've heard the alarm or not, increasing the odds that the intruder will choose to leave as soon as the alarm sounds. Packaged and integrated garage systems are on the market, some that transmit a wireless signal that activates an alert / siren device inside your home that you are more likely to hear. Some systems will even call a pre-programmed telephone number, such as your cell phone, in the event of intrusion. Do not program 9-1-1 or you local police department number into these devices. Unlike true monitored systems, no-one will verify if the alarm is true of false, and law enforcement may respond unnecessarily. In some locales this practice may result in a fine or other penalties.

Garage Door Closing Systems

An open and unattended garage door is a strong invitation to thieves. The best security practice is to always close and lock your garage door unless you are entering, exiting, or occupying the garage. However, if you occasionally (or habitually) forget to close your garage door, an automatic closing device is worth consideration. These devices close the garage door after it has remained open for a pre-determined period of time. Virtually all models include an over-ride feature should you wish to work in the garage or need to have the door open for some other reason.

If you install an automatic closing system, make sure you have a functioning, infrared safety system (required in most areas) that prevents the door from closing if someone is in the door path. Doors lacking such sensors pose a serious safety hazard, particularly if small children play in the area. Note that these sensors will not prevent the door from closing if someone (criminal or not) is well within the garage. A windowless, detached garage without heating or air-conditioning can become a death trap for anyone unable to exit the garage. While many garage doors have emergency latches that open the door from within, a child or someone with a disability may not be able to operate it. The best practice is to manually close or wait for the door to automatically close before departing. Additionally, reduce the safety risks by setting the door to allow just enough time to exit the garage prior to auto-closing. This also reduces the odds that a thief -- or an innocent child -- will have a brief opportunity to slip into the still-open garage after you've driven away.

Garage Clutter

Some keep their garages neat and clean, others use them as dumping grounds for items they don't want inside the house. A cluttered garage with piles of storage boxes offers hiding places for thieves or other criminals. Keep your garage organized; ensure there is no area large enough for a person to hide that can't be viewed from inside your vehicle or from any garage entryway. You do not wish to find yourself surprised and trapped inside a closed garage with a criminal intruder.

Shed and Tool Security

It's not surprising sheds are frequent burglary targets. Sheds are unoccupied and often house items of value. Even simple garden tools left in the shed, such as a spade or a hand trowel, can facilitate forced entry into your home. A shed is also unlikely to be monitored by an alarm.

Shed construction quality varies greatly, from wood or corrugated sheet metal structures with unframed doors to expensive, high-security, galvanized steel sheds anchored on concrete pads. If you have anything short of a high security shed, there's rarely any point in spending a fortune on lock security. It's too easy to pry apart shed panels or exploit other weaknesses in simple shed structures.

Still,a padlock alone may ward off some thieves. Thieves must defeat the lock or break or force some part of the shed, and some thieves prefer quick, unforced entry. Even if caught in the act, a thief that did not forcibly enter a shed might avoid charges by claiming they heard a noise or had some other cause to enter. A lock will also help prevent you from walking in on a crime in progress. A broken, open or missing lock may warn you that something is amiss. Don't enter a shed under these circumstances until you are certain no one is inside.

Shed doors frequently feature a hasp and pin lock or similar, simple locking mechanism that accepts a padlock. Secure shed doors with a heavy-duty, hardened, commercial padlock with a shrouded shackle (see illustration). A shrouded shackle padlock makes it difficult to position bolt cutter blades to cut the bolt, and a hardened lock will be difficult to cut or saw. Don't seek elegance; use the largest padlock your lock will accept. If the hasp or bolt lock components can be removed from outside the shed

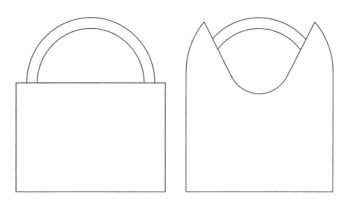

The padlock on the right features a shrouded shackle design. Note how the body of this lock surrounds the bolt and makes it harder to position tools to cut the bolt.

with a screwdriver or other simple tools, secure these components to the shed and shed door with tamper-proof screws or bolts. Remember that few padlocks can withstand a well-equipped attack. Furthermore, if a light-duty shed is secured with a lock, even a poorly equipped thief may successfully attack the shed structure, door hinges or anchoring instead of the lock. A padlock is an essential step, but your best option is to keep little of value stored in any standard shed, and to make sure property stored in a shed falls under your homeowner's insurance policy.

Additional shed and tool security measures:

▶ Light the area around your shed after dark.

▶ Screw or nail any shed windows closed and cover tools or machinery with a tarp to reduce visual temptation.

▶ Even a flimsy shed can benefit from a simple open-or-shut magnetic alarm in addition to a padlock. These battery-operated alarms can make enough noise to alert you and frighten thieves. Even if the intruder doesn't immediately run due to the alarm noise, they may hurry to avoid capture and therefore get away with less property.

▶ Never leave tools, such as hammers, screwdrivers, or pliers lying about outside. This not only avoids theft of these items but also prevents use of them as tools to break into your home. Store these tools in locked tool chests or storage bins inside a locked garage or within the home. Make a clean-up walk after you work on an outdoor project. It's easy to leave a screwdriver or other small tool on a window ledge or other handy "set-down" point while focusing on a job.

▶ Keep ladders in a garage or within the residence. Aside from the potential loss of the ladder, there's no benefit in offering a thief easy access to second story doors, windows or rooftops.

▶ If your shed features a framed door (i.e., looks and operates much like a household door), use a good lock set or a dead-bolt lock. Secure the lock strike plates as firmly as possible to the shed structure.

Fences, Gates and Patios

Fences have some deterrence value, but even a very high fence won't stop an athletic intruder.

Remember, though, that any security barriers may be better than none. A high fence with a locked gate might be enough of a nuisance to deter some thieves. Strong fences and gates with high-security locks might force a thief to abandon fragile stolen property (such as computer equipment that can't be easily tossed over the fence), or to use an exit that offers less concealment. Note that locked fences may require you to schedule access for legitimate service or utility workers.

Use passive measures to reduce the appeal of climbing your fence. Weak, wooden or plastic trellises attached to the top of a fence (if permitted in your neighborhood) can force a thief to make noise; the trellis won't support body weight. Thorny, climbing vines or similar plants can make your fence very unpleasant to scale. Check with your local nursery for species that thrive in your region but won't invade your neighbor's property. Thorny bushes, cactus or other defensive plants around the fence and/or patio perimeter provide additional obstacles.

If you are installing a new fence, consider fence materials. Solid fences serve as effective privacy walls, but also provide "privacy" to any thief outside. Iron fences and gates are sturdy and offer a clear view of anyone beyond the fence. An iron gate with a quality lock takes time to defeat, particularly if you weld the hinge pins in place. A secondary lock in addition to the primary latch lock adds yet another time-consuming obstacle for intruders. Unfortunately, iron fences are expensive. A six-foot tall, chain link fence (or even a wooden picket fence) is a less expensive, albeit less secure, alternative. Understand that all but climb-and-cut-resistant, high-security fences or meshes offer only minimal property protection. Furthermore, most high-security fences aren't designed for visual appeal and are primarily used in commercial applications.

For most residences, relying on fences to protect your yard, courtyard or property within is unwise. Many residents leave expensive gas grills (complete with wheels for portability) on the back porch or patio. Use a padlock and high security chain to lock grills or other valuable outdoor property to a sturdy structure or to a mature tree. Alternatively, use of a long cable or chain to lock property such as grills, bicycles, tables and chairs together. If a thief lacks cutting tools, they may be unable to carry away the property.

Finally, bicycles are routinely stolen. An unattended and unsecured bike offers both a theft opportunity and the getaway transportation. Lock your bikes at all times, even when you leave them for just a moment in your own backyard.

CHAPTER 8
Burglar Alarms

Overview and Benefits

Alarms are deterrent and warning devices. They do not physically prevent forced or unforced entry, nor do they allow you to safely disregard or fail to use other common-sense security measures. Provided you understand these points, alarm systems can play an important role in overall home security.

A professionally recommended and installed security system, if consistently used, provides a much greater chance that a forced entry will be aborted should the alarm sound. If you are in the residence, an alarm system may provide priceless warning of a threat to your personal safety. Moreover, many modern "burglar alarm" systems also include fire alarms, panic alarms and other functions. The peace of mind that may result from implementing the additional layers of protection a modern alarm system offers can be well worth the cost.

Alarms generally arm in one of two modes: home/stay or away. This is useful primarily if your alarm includes motion sensors or other interior monitoring devices. When no-one is in the home, the "away" mode activates all sensors on the alarm system. If you are in the home, the "home or stay" mode activates only door, window or exterior sensors. Motion sensing devices, for example, would not be activated in this case, allowing you to move about within the home while enjoying the protection of the system.

Convenience features, such as door, chime or "child" monitoring, are useful even when an alarm is unarmed. If this feature is active and a door or window that is integrated into the system is opened or closed (perhaps by a straying toddler), a chime sounds inside the home, but no alarm is triggered.

Understand the difference between monitored and un-monitored alarm systems. *Monitored* alarm systems, if triggered, send an immediate signal to the alarm company's dispatch center. In response to the signal, an alarm company operator calls your home or cell phone to learn whether the alarm is accidental or real. If the alarm is false or accidental, the homeowner provides the monitoring company with a predetermined password known only to the homeowner, the homeowner's household members, and the alarm company representatives. Un-monitored systems do not send signals beyond any sirens, bells or lights that are configured to go off if the alarm is triggered.

Monitored alarm systems safeguard against a variety of circumstances. If an intruder ignores a triggered alarm and has you under their control, you're not on your own. The alarm company will call, and whether you attempt to pacify the thief by pretending to offer a legitimate password (the thief won't know), cry for help, or don't answer the phone at all, the alarm company will dispatch police to the home.

Should an intruder force you to disarm the alarm through the keypad, most systems allow you to enter a pre-determined, emergency code. Using this code appears to fully deactivated the alarm. In reality, you have sent an urgent, silent call for help to monitoring company personnel who immediately dispatch police to your residence. This type of alert generally receives high priority, as it indicates an intruder (likely armed) is presently in the home and is in control of and threatening the resident or residents with bodily harm or deadly force.

Unless you absolutely cannot afford it, a monitored alarm has enormous advantages over an un-monitored system. Although an un-monitored alarm may warn you of a break-in, summoning help is up to you. If an intruder is in the home, you may be unable to call for help. A monitored system makes the call for you.

Alarm System Basics

There are five primary components to an alarm system.

> ▶   *The Alarm Box.* This is the "brain" of the system, and all other components connect to or have wireless contact with the box. The consumer rarely needs to deal with this component.

> ▶   *The Keypad.* The keypad is the command center of the alarm system. Residents use the keypad to activate and deactivate the alarm, to change passwords, settings and other functions, or to call for emergency help with a single push of a button. The keypad also communicates the current status of the system (i.e., armed or not) and if the system detects any problems or malfunctions in sensors or other components.

> ▶   *The Sensors.* These devices employ a variety of mechanical, electrical and optical means to detect if someone is attempting to break in or has broken into your dwelling.

> ▶   *The Alarm Alert.* A siren or other loud device that sounds to indicate a sensor has been triggered. Monitored systems also send an automatic alert signal to an alarm monitoring dispatch center.

> ▶   *The Power Backup System.* This system supplies temporary power to your alarm system in the event of an electrical outage. Note that some systems do not have this feature and may not function during power outages.

Keypad Considerations

Keypads are your command and control centers for the alarm system. Keypad

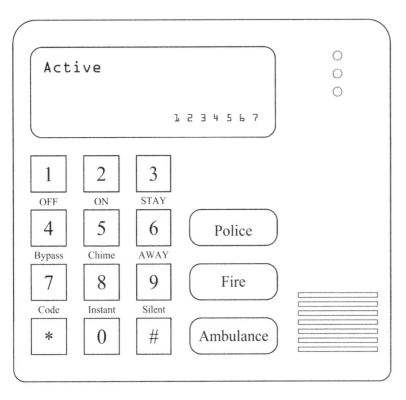

The keypad controls all alarm functions. Designs vary, so make certain you understand how to use all the features of your system.

designs vary significantly, so you must learn all the operational particulars of any alarm you purchase or inherit when you move into a new residence. The keypad activates, changes, or deactivates virtually all functions of the system. Many functions require a pass-code, most often a series of 4 digits, in order to operate. Most keypads consist of a numeric pad, an LCD or other window to display alarm information, and other buttons or indicators depending on the system.

Physical placement of the keypad(s) is important, particularly if you have a panic button function that sends an immediate, silent alarm to a police dispatcher. If you need this function, you'll need it quickly. Modern systems easily accommodate multiple keypads. One keypad situated near the main exit door and a second in the master bedroom increases your signaling options during an intrusion and add system convenience.

Keypads should never be located where they are visible from outside. Thieves will look through windows to determine if your alarm system is armed. You don't want this to happen on the one day you forget to set your system.

Sensor Types and Applications

While it's not necessary to become an alarm or electronics expert, it is helpful to be familiar with the most commonly used alarm system sensors. You'll be more comfortable discussing alarm systems with potential installers, and the foreknowledge will speed you through the shopping process, as your representative can spend more time focusing on your specific needs rather than on device functionality.

▶ Magnetic (wired or wireless) sensors. You needn't understand the electrical theory; simply know that alarm systems can detect whether or not two magnetic sensor components are aligned. The components mount on doors, windows, and corresponding frames so that they come into alignment when these doors or windows are fully closed. Opening the doors or windows moves the magnets out of alignment and triggers an alarm. Magnetic sensors (and other sensor types) perform an additional function. Should you attempt to arm the alarm with a door or window ajar, the alarm system will sense that these entries are not secure. The system will not arm or will arm only if you choose to over-ride these sensors.

▶ Motion detectors. These sensors detect physical motion or, depending on sensor type, heat changes in the sensor path. Motion detectors are used inside homes to detect intruders, but are also commonly found in exterior applications, primarily to turn on floodlights in driveways or walkways if someone approaches. A single motion detector can cover a large room, and they are sometimes used in lieu of magnetic sensors on every single window or door to reduce system cost. Think this approach through carefully; motion sensors are generally not active when the alarm is armed in the "home" or "stay" mode. You'll receive no alert if an intruder enters through a door or window that lacks a sensor if "stay" mode is active. However, if your primary concern is burglary when you are away from home, several well-positioned motion detectors can cover all entrances and every room in your home. Unfortunately, not all intruders seek entry to an unoccupied house. Rapists often seek residences occupied by women living alone, and other violent offenders simply may not care whether a home is occupied or not. Therefore, while motion sensors are useful, install sensors on as many entry ways into the household as possible to prevent undetected intrusion. Finally, if you have pets that remain indoors when you are out of the home, check with your alarm provider before installing motion sensors. Adjustable motion sensors may allow detection of a human moving about, but effectively "ignore" the movement of pets.

▶   Beam Sensors use an infrared or photoelectric light beam. Two components are required, one to send the beam, the other to receive it. Interrupting the beam, however briefly, triggers an alarm. This method has limitations, as there must be a direct line of sight between the two sensors and intruders may notice and avoid the beam. You've probably seen examples of this in movies about bank or jewelry heists, where thieves cautiously move through a room riddled with photo-beam alarm circuits. Beam sensors work both in stand-alone applications and in support of other devices. If an intruder breaks, cuts, or removes a large pane of glass, for example, they may be able to enter the residence without opening the sash. Magnetic sensors and window locks are bypassed, but a concealed beam sensor across this path of entry will still trigger the alarm system.

▶   Glass Break Sensors react to the acoustic properties generated by the sound of shattering glass. These alarms are useful but not perfect. The mount must be reasonably close to the windows you wish to protect. Barking dogs and other loud noises may set them off. A variant, seismic glass alarms mount directly to window glazing and detect movement or vibration to signal window tampering. These alarms are prone to trigger during thunderstorms or from other, loud noises that rattle the windows.

Shopping and Evaluating Systems

Start by talking to several alarm companies so that you can compare features and pricing. Ask for references, including current customers, and follow up by contacting some references. It is import to deal only with a reputable, experienced company. Let newcomers, novices and start-ups test their skills and products on someone else.

Ask for a sales representative to visit your home and give you an estimate. They should survey the premises and recommend the best way to monitor doors, windows and other vulnerable areas. If their initial quote is beyond your means, ask about the availability of simpler systems that would still provide you with significant security improvement.

Alarm companies routinely offer "packages" at an attractive price. These packages typically offer a basic system that includes the alarm box, a power backup system, sirens or alerts, and anywhere from three to six installed sensors. While this may fully cover a small apartment, it may leave a two or three bedroom home with windows or areas that aren't protected by the system. A direct sensor on every exterior door and window in your residence is ideal, but installing additional sensors rapidly adds to package prices. Consider your "at home" situation first, as your personal safety is more valuable than any property you might lose. If an alarm system does nothing else, it should either scare away intruders or give anyone inside the home a warning that a crime is in progress. At minimum, you should seek "at home" or "stay" mode alarm sensing for all doors that lead into the house, all bathroom and children's room windows, and of windows (as many as you can possibly afford) not visible from the street. For any proposed design, ask your alarm company representative what illegal entry possibilities aren't covered by the system. Don't accept vague answers or responses like "your key areas" are covered. Make sure you fully understand which doors, windows or other avenues remain vulnerable to undetected entry *when you are at home* with the system armed. Remember that some sensors, such as motion detectors, won't activate when you arm the system at home. You may indeed have "full" coverage when you are *away from home* with a few magnetic entry sensors and several motion detectors. If you are in the home and the motion detectors are deactivated, your coverage may be substantially less.

Should your system ultimately leave some rooms or windows unprotected, you'll at least be aware of it so that you can take additional precautions. Use appropriate locking devices, Charley bars, surveillance or any of the other measures described in this book to protect the areas your alarm system does not cover.

Alarm Purchasing Checklist

▶ What areas of the residence are and are NOT covered in both home and away modes.

▶ How does the system function in a power outage?

▶ Is there a backup battery system and how long will it operate? Note that power outages, especially if lengthy, are prime opportunities for burglars who know that most alarms, lights and other defensive systems are down.

▶ How often does the backup battery needs changing and at what cost?

▶ Does the system have or support all the features you desire?

▶ Does the system have the capacity to handle additional sensors or security measures if you decide to add them later?

▶ Has the sales representative undergone training in the security field and/or have relevant experience?

▶ Does the company uses their own installers or contractors? Do installers go through company training prior to or upon hiring?

▶ Who will train you on alarm system use? If not the sales representative, does the instructor have training or qualifications to instruct on alarm operation?

▶ How do false alarm incident rates for your alarm company compare to competitors? This is an important financial consideration, as in many areas cities or counties charge for responses to false alarms.

▶ What are the ongoing fees for monitoring, and what are the contractual obligations (such as the minimum number of months you guarantee to pay for monitoring)?

▶ What warranties or guarantees cover the system hardware and monitoring service?

▶ Does the contract include maintenance? If not, is a maintenance agreement available?

▶ Will the alarm company obtain any permits required by your local city or county? If permits are your obligation, ask whether the alarm company provides instructive support as you obtain the required permits.

▶ Will the alarm system qualify you for insurance premium discounts?

Verify the last item with your insurance agent, not alarm company personnel.

Before you sign paperwork confirming that the system installation is complete, make sure you understand:

- ▶ All the functions of your alarm system – not just how to arm or disarm it

- ▶ How often the system needs testing and how to perform testing

- ▶ What to do in the event of a false alarm

- ▶ What to do in the event of a real emergency

- ▶ Your alarm codes and how to change them

- ▶ Your telephone password or personal code and use of these codes

- ▶ Where to call if you have additional questions or concerns

CHAPTER 9
Exterior Visibility

Property Review

Yards or property that offer dark, shadowy places create security issues. Intruders may safely hide and survey the area and the home, and to wait for an entry time of their choosing. For security purposes, you want the clearest, most unobstructed view of your property possible (from within your residence), and you want this view both day and at night. You especially want this same, clear view around any doors you use for entry. Take a good look at your property from both inside the house and outside and ask yourself these questions

▶   Does anything, perhaps part of the house, a detached garage or shed, landscaping features or other items partially or totally obstruct the view of some areas of your property?

▶   Are narrow passageways, such as a spaces between the house and a fence, visible from your interior windows? Often a wooden or stone "privacy" fence, offers equal privacy to an intruder who can use the fence to hide from the street, the neighbors, and the home occupants.

▶   Are approaches to your doorways readily visible, or could someone hide near the entrance?

▶   Is your entire driveway visible from the street entrance? Can you see the driveway from both inside and outside the garage, or from any other area where you park?

Landscaping

Lush landscaping adds beauty and value to property. Yet bushes and shrubs, particularly if planted close to buildings, can also offer an excellent hiding place for thieves. You don't have to bulldoze and pave your surroundings, but do regularly keep bushes and shrubs neatly trimmed with an eye towards property visibility. Some evergreens and a few deciduous trees grow branches that droop downwards and may offer a lot of cover beneath the tree. Trim and clear away any branches or foliage less than six feet from the ground. Landscaping materials, such as mulch piles should be low enough to offer no cover.

Outdoor Objects

A couple in a suburban neighborhood kept a large, municipal trash bin near the garage and next to a side entrance to the home. The bin was large enough and placed in such a way that a criminal was able to hide behind the bin as the couple arrived home. They parked in the driveway, exited the vehicle and unlocked the door of the home. The intruder, hiding just feet from the doorway, simply stepped into the home and robbed them at gunpoint. The victims' alarm system was active but of no help. The built-in, sixty second delay between door opening and alarm triggering was more than enough time to commit aggravated robbery. The bin placement was dangerous. Furthermore, the couple failed to look behind or around the bin before exiting the vehicle.

Keep any items large enough to conceal a person against a fence or a wall, or in a corner that offers a good view of the remaining exposed sides. Preferably, store such objects away from entrances to the home and away from any area where people routinely enter or exit vehicles.

Sometimes property layout does not offer ideal placement locations. Fortunately technologies, both old and new, can assist you.

Mirrors

You've certainly seen convex, "fish-eye" mirrors, such as those used in department stores to monitor store activity. These mirrors are available from security supply merchants and from mirror distributors or manufacturers. Properly positioned, these mirrors offer a good view of problem areas, such as behind garages or sheds, or around blind corners from almost any vantage point you desire. They don't require electrical wiring or batteries, and it's easy to determine if someone has tampered with them.

These are particularly useful if "blind spots" exist around garage doorways or where you enter or exit the home. A routine check in a well-placed mirror can prevent anyone from taking you by surprise. Also see: Chapter 10, Security Surveillance.

Address Markers

When you think about exterior visibility, you're usually concerned about your own ability to see your property, as well as making it clear to potential intruders that they can be seen by you. However, in the event you need emergency help, it's essential that police or other first-responders be able to easily see *you*. Home addresses often aren't easy to read from the street. Display your house or home number prominently on the home structure in large, easy-to-read figures. Trim or move bushes, trees, or other objects that block or obscure the house number. Light the house number so that it is easy to read from the street at night. If you live in a single-family home and your sub-division allows it, paint your address on the curb in front of your home in a spot where parked cars won't block visibility. Paint approximately a 6"x 8" white rectangle, and over-paint the address number or letters in large, black, block-style type (stencils are readily available). This technique produces high contrast and is easy to read both day and night.

CHAPTER 10
Security Surveillance

Benefits and Costs

Once an expensive proposition, consumer surveillance cameras and system costs declined dramatically over the past decade thanks to advances in digital technology. Many home surveillance systems now tie directly into the internet or a personal computer (PC), allowing you to monitor any or all of the system's camera views on your computer from within the home or, often, from a remote location. Note that apartment regulations may limit or prohibit installation of cameras outside your unit.

Total system cost depends on the number of cameras needed, the capabilities and the quality of the components. Consumer grade packages are available in discount stores, and many offer excellent value. Commercial grade systems are typically hardier and may offer better visuals and additional features, but cost thousands of dollars more.

Split-screen monitoring, video recording, color imagery, low-light capabilities and a growing host of specialty features can quickly increase the price. As of this writing, basic, pre-packaged consumer systems cost from under $500 to over $1500. This figure does not include installation.

You may want cameras inside your home as well as outside. If you use a surveillance system to monitor the interior of your home for security purposes (or perhaps to keep an eye on a baby-sitter or house cleaner), be sure you understand your local laws. Some areas prohibit videotaping without providing a notice.

Although many consumer grade, packaged systems advertise easy self-installation, this is predicated on some level of mechanical, technical and computer savvy, particularly if the system ties into a local area computer network or a PC. If you lack the knowledge or skills, use a reputable and qualified installer.

Some of the advantages of video surveillance include:

▶ Convenience: You may be able to see who is at the front door, for example, without leaving the back of the home.

▶ Deterrence: Visible video cameras may ward off thieves who are not eager to have their images captured. A number of inexpensive yet realistic looking, phony cameras are available if deterrence is the only goal.

▶ Warning: You may have a visual forewarning of suspicious or criminal activity. This is especially true in systems with multiple cameras covering much of the home perimeter.

▶ Evidence: Systems equipped with recorders may capture video of a burglar or thief whether you are home or away.

Note: Surveillance cameras and mirrors, as described in Chapter 9, are not mutually exclusive. You can use a combination of the two to achieve full property visibility while controlling costs.

System Components and Considerations

The variety of consumer surveillance systems, capabilities, cameras, recorders, monitors and associated devices is vast and grows daily. The price disparity between consumer and commercial grade cameras and hardware intimidates and confuses some buyers. If you know what you're looking for, the shopping process is easier. Ascertain surveillance needs for your property layout by considering the following:

▶ How many cameras do you need? Although most surveillance cameras offer a wide-angle view, they can't see around corners or through objects. Diagram your property and think about the minimum number of cameras required for you to view the areas you want to observe. You may decide you don't need a four-camera (or larger) system if windows permit you to view most areas outside of your home.

▶ Do the cameras need to function well at night or in areas that receive little light? If so, you need low light cameras, or cameras that use infrared LEDs to "illuminate" an area.

▶ Where will you place cameras? Do you need to run wires over a long distance or through difficult attic access spaces? Can you easily reach, install, and mount cameras in spots that will capture a good view of the areas you want to monitor?

▶ Hard-wired or wireless: which fits your needs and budget? Wireless cameras install almost anywhere within a reasonable range of the residence without extensive stringing of wires and connectors. However, wireless cameras have disadvantages. Wireless camera signals may be susceptible to interference from wireless Internet networks or similar devices. It's also possible for others to intercept a wireless camera signal, allowing them to watch activity in or on the property. Finally, wireless cameras operate on battery power and therefore require attention to battery strength and life.

▶ Do you need or want a fixed and dedicated viewing monitor? Some systems don't require dedicated monitors, but stream video via the web. This enables you to access the camera views from almost any computer anywhere, but also requires that a computer be running whenever you wish to use the surveillance system.

▶   Do you require a color system, or is black and white sufficient? Cinema quality imagery is nice, but unnecessary for home applications. Black and white cameras are cheaper than color, for example, and often have better tolerance for low light conditions. Conversely, identifying clothing color might help police apprehend a suspect in the event of a crime or attempted crime caught on camera.

▶   What resolution meets your needs? You want camera and/or monitor resolution sufficient to recognize if individuals on your property belong there or not. Resolution, usually measured by the number of horizontal and vertical pixels (i.e., 720x480) continues to improve with advancing technology. Older analog models may describe resolution in scan lines. You needn't understand or focus on these numbers. See for yourself what the picture images look like for any system you consider purchasing. If you don't buy a pre-packaged system or are adding to an existing system, make sure the resolution of all the system components are compatible.

▶   If your property is large, is one view at a time sufficient? Many systems are capable of simultaneous, multi-camera displays. This means your monitor or computer screen divides into two, four, or more sections, each displaying the image from a different camera. Other multi-camera systems may alternate between cameras, providing full-screen images for a few seconds before switching to the next camera in sequence. You'll want the ability to select a specific camera view, as well. If you spot suspicious activity, a full screen view from the appropriate camera makes it much easier to determine what's going on.

▶   Do you need a Digital video recorder (DVR)? A DVR records and saves the camera signals so they may be played later, perhaps for police. Hard drive storage technology has advanced to the degree that many hours of video store easily on a single hard drive or other device. Some systems use motion detectors to activate recording for a pre-set period of time, or for as long as motion is detected in the camera's field of view. Others are continuously active and utilize time lapse photography, saving a picture every second or two. Many current systems are available with an integrated DVR device; No other computer or hardware is needed for recording. Other systems require a running PC or laptop to serve as a DVR. A DVR isn't essential if you simply wish to see outside your home, but can be of great evidential use to police or prosecutors in the event of a robbery or burglary.

▶ Do you prefer to hide your exterior cameras or leave them visible? Thieves don't like to be caught on camera, so a visible camera system can deter crime. In fact, you can buy realistic looking dummy security cameras that provide the illusion of an in-place surveillance system. A disadvantage of visible cameras is that determined thieves may see and break or disable one or more cameras, particularly if they are certain you are not within the home. Additionally if criminals enter your home and are aware of your surveillance system, they will try to locate and steal or destroy DVR devices. Low profile camera designs are available if you opt for a less-than-obvious system. Although it's difficult to make a camera completely invisible, many models are quite small and offer ingenious mounting methods or disguises that require a careful eye to notice. Place any interior monitoring cameras (so-called nanny cams) discretely. Any DVR or recording system should be out of sight and, preferably, locked away or otherwise secured.

The variety of affordable surveillance devices grows daily. Video doorbells, nanny-cams, baby monitors and dozens of other products fill many, specific needs. How do you choose? As a general rule, if you feel unsafe when you exit the home into specific areas in or around your property, these areas merit remote surveillance consideration.

When you comparison shop for surveillance systems, consider installation issues along with system features and capabilities. Many of the systems on the market are suitable for home installation with minimal mechanical or technical skills, but others require electrical or computer savvy. While many handy-persons might be happy to handle the job for you, it's often worth the small extra expense to hire a reputable security firm to install surveillance systems. The fewer individuals that are aware of and understand your system -- and the more trusted these individuals are -- the better.

CHAPTER 11
Exterior Lighting

Statistically, a burglary takes place in the United States every 14.5 seconds. A majority of these burglaries occur during the day, but close to a third of residential burglaries take place at night when it's far more likely that you'll be home. That's more than enough to warrant specific, night time protective efforts, and exterior lighting plays a primary role

The Role of Lighting in Security

Visual acuity diminishes under low light conditions. Well-lit property does more than help you see and identify visitors outside your door at night. Light poses an unmistakable deterrent to burglars. Whether you are home or not, well lit property makes it much more likely that occupants or neighbors will see an intruder approach, lurk about, or break in to a residence. Eliminate darkness or shadows across your property to keep this deterrent value in place.

Survey your property from inside and outside (take a flashlight) at night. Can you approach the home, from any direction, in a way that keeps you largely in darkness or shadows? Is your residence the darkest on the street on in your complex? Either of these conditions should be corrected.

Before lighting up your property like a sports stadium, consider how the placement of lights might affect your neighbors. Though they'll likely appreciate that you're concerned about neighborhood security, but may not be as grateful if you shine bright floodlights directly at their bedroom windows.

In addition to your private lighting, routinely notice municipal street lamps or other city lighting and promptly report any outages to the proper agency.

Common Security Light Devices

There are many types of exterior lighting options, ranging from motion-activated floodlights, to low-voltage, in-ground path lighting, to simple porch lights.

WARNING: do not install electrical devices unless you have the skills or qualifications to do so. Beyond the immediate personal danger (the majority of these devices require 120 volt / 15 amp household current), improper wiring may cause the devices to fail, or may overload a circuit causing many devices or outlets to fail, or create a fire hazard. Light installation is usually a reasonably affordable, simple and straightforward job for a qualified electrician.

You can meet most security lighting needs with one or more of the following devices:

Motion Detector Lights

These lights activate by detecting motion. The motion detector, often an infrared sensor, is integrated into the fixture. If a person, vehicle or object moves within the path of the sensor, the lights turn on and remain on for a period of time preset by the resident, usually between one to thirty minutes. Motion activated lights are commonly used to illuminate entrance areas for two reasons. First, they help clearly see any night time callers outside the entrance. Second, they'll activate if *you* approach your residence, allowing you to clearly see the area, your keys, and the lock. Use caution when exiting the home. Exterior motion-sensor lights may not activate from your own motion until you're well outside the doorway. There's always the possibility that you didn't notice the lights previously activate (and later switch off per the timer preset) as an intruder approached - an intruder now hiding, motionless, near your entry. Always use either a secondary light with an interior switch, or install a manual over-ride switch, to operate the motion-activated floodlights so that you may clearly see the area surrounding the exit before you leave the residence. Motion detector fixtures popularly use floodlights, as they are bright and cover a wide area. Sun-

light sensors built into most modern fixtures over-ride the motion detector during the day and prevent the light from turning on and off unnecessarily.

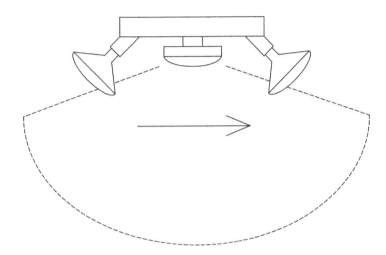

Always use a fixture with at least two floodlights so that the system functions if one lamp burns out. Be certain to replace any burned-out lamps immediately to preserve this redundant protection.

A pair of motion activated floodlights power-fully illuminate dark driveways or corners. Most motion devices best detect motion across, not towards the sensor, so place fixtures accordingly.

As noted, there are times when you may wish to over-ride the motion sensor and turn on the light from inside the home. Perhaps you hear a noise outside, but you note that your motion sensor light did not activate and want to double-check. Modern models allow you to over-ride the motion sensor, typically by double-flipping a designated, wired switch. That's of no help if the over-ride switch isn't located inside the home. Before you or a professional install lighting fixtures, make sure you've determined which fixtures need to be wired to turn on from within the home. Models vary and aren't always intuitive, so make sure you understand how to over-ride your specific fixtures. If you have an older model, or if your unit is not wired to an interior switch, install a secondary light fixture with an interior switch.

Most current sensors are better at sensing movement across the sensor path than directly towards or away from it. Many individuals mount motion sensor lights centered over their garage door and pointed towards the driveway. Such placement works well for detecting motion across the driveway, but is less sensitive detecting motion up the driveway -- yet this may be the most likely motion you want to detect. With these sensor limitations in mind, carefully consider the area you want to monitor and the direction of likely approach. Place your lights and sensor facing as close as possible to 90° degrees relative to the monitored pathway.

Separate light fixtures and sensor modules are necessary for some property layouts. For example, the best way to monitor the entrance to your home may be to point the sensor directly across your driveway. Suppose a combination sensor/lamp fixture aimed in this direction, even when properly adjusted, shines into your neighbor's windows. A fixture wired to a separate, remote sensor -- readily available and inexpensive -- solves the problem. Mount the sensor where you need it, and mount the lights in position to illuminate the area without blinding the neighbors. Additional wiring is required, but the very effective and neighbor-friendly result is worth the effort.

Most motion activated lighting sensors feature a sensitivity adjustment. Reduce the sensitivity too much, and the lights may not turn on unless a burglar stands in front of the sensor waving their arms. If set too sensitive, you may have the visual equivalent of a flashing neon sign. Neither you nor your neighbors are likely to appreciate this. Adjust, test and repeat until the fixture functions properly.

Stray cats or dogs, blowing leaves or other harmless items all can set off a sensitive motion detector, but there are a steps you can take to avoid unwanted triggers:

➤ Reduce the range of your sensor so that it only covers the area you desire. Most sensors detect motion out to about 70 feet, and some models are range adjustable.   If there is no built-in range adjustment, tilting the sensor more towards the ground will reduce the range. You can test the range by walking across the sensor path at different distances.

▶   Carefully aim your sensor across the specific path you want to monitor. Sensors usually cover a broad area of about 240 degrees. If you need to narrow the range, you can use thick tape, such as duct tape, to mask one or both sides of the sensor to reduce the sensing band width.

▶   Trim back low hanging tree or bush limbs that are in the sensor path. Regardless of sensitivity settings, a leafy branch swinging in the breeze is sure to trigger the light.

Photo-sensitive Lights

Lighting units with photo-voltaic sensors detect low light conditions (nighttime or even strong rainstorms) and activate the lamp. Use these units in areas that you wish to illuminate each and every night, all night long.   You may not even need to buy a special photo-sensitive light fixture. Severable available floodlight lamps have a sensor built in to the bulb base. Just screw these lamps into an existing socket.

Photo lights add convenience; you don't have to remember to turn them on or off. It's also readily evident when a photo-sensitive lamp is burnt out or not functioning. On the downside, photosensitive lights consume more electricity than do motion detector systems as the lamps remain on all night.

Timer Lights

Unlike exterior motion or photo sensitive fixtures, timers generally aren't built into the light fixture. The timer is a separate device wired into the light circuit. Some units replace standard, existing, wall-mounted light switches with a combination timer and switch device. Existing light fixtures -- or anything else operated by the switch -- may be programmed to turn on or off via the timer switch.

Most timing devices turn the lights off and on at specific, user designated times. More elaborate timers calculate sunrise and sunset times based on where you live and on the calendar date. The lights turn on at sunset and off at dusk, automatically adjusting for seasonal changes and even for daylight savings time. These sunrise-sunset timers are useful, as you don't have to remember to periodically adjust the timer settings. Some models will randomly vary the exact on-off times by an hour or so based around sunset and sunrise. This feature gives the strong impression that a person, not a device, is turning the light on and off, indicating that the home must be occupied.

Light Planning

Theatrical lighting designers divide stages into "areas" at the very beginning of the design process. While you don't need theatrical precision, dividing your exterior property into manageable regions will make planning your lighting needs easier.

Make a rough pencil outline of your property (top down view). Mark door, window, garage and shed locations. Note any trees, shrubs or objects that are currently in shadow or cast a shadow. Remember that additional lighting may create new shadows. Use a strong flashlight or portable floodlight on your property at night to see if your planned light placement might result in new visibility problems.

Next, review the following priorities. Each of these areas should be well lit, although it's fine if a single light source adequately covers several regions.

Outdoor Lighting Priorities

- ▶ Entry doors and surrounding areas

- ▶ Steps and pathways leading to and around your home

- ▶ Any side of the home that is in shadow, cannot be fully viewed from inside the home, or is protected by a privacy fence.

- ▶ Driveways, garage doors, and areas surrounding garages

- ▶ Decks, porches, and patios

- ▶ Dark or shadowy areas large enough to conceal a person

Mount lighting or sensing devices at least eight feet from the ground when possible. At this height, the average individual can't unscrew the lamp or tamper with fixtures without a step stool or some other assistance. Use floodlights with enough wattage or lumen output to fully light the target area. It's not necessary to recreate daylight; some small areas require surprisingly low-wattage bulbs and little energy consumption to illuminate adequately for you to see. Decide which, if any areas you wish to illuminate all night long. Exterior doors, exterior areas around children's room windows, driveways and back porches or terraces are candidates for all-night illumination. Use photosensitive fixtures or timer devices for these areas. For areas where all-night illumination is undesired, motion-activated fixtures are ideal.

In both cases (photosensitive or motion-sensor illumination), automation is an asset. Timed, photosensitive and motion-sensor lights will turn on and off, day in and day out, whether you're home or not. These devices don't provide any clues regarding home occupancy.

All the fixture types discussed are available for incandescent floodlights, but you may live in a rural area or have a large piece of property that stretches the limits of

92

A Sample Lighting Diagram

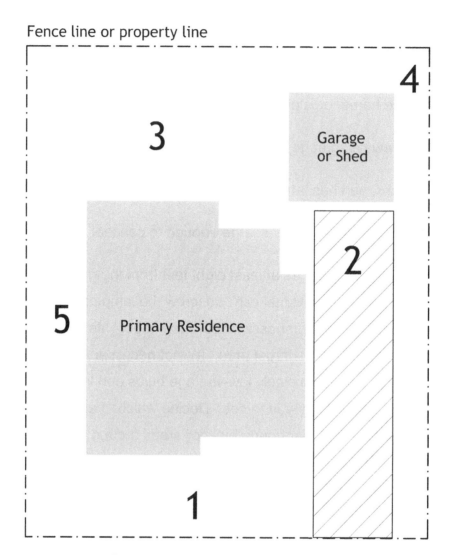

Street / Front of Home

Divide property into lighting groups or regions. In this case area 1, 2 and 3 (front, back and driveway) merit at least some lighting that automatically illuminates at sunset. For areas 4 and 5 (behind an outbuilding and in a passway along the fence), motion activated lights will discourage activity in these less-than-visible from the home areas.

incandescent lamps. In urban settings, you may wish to better illuminate your property in a manner that saves energy and is less likely to bother neighbors. Either of these issues can be solved with various lamp and system options.

Lamp Types and Low Voltage Systems

▶ Incandescent floodlights are inexpensive and are sold in many hardware and grocery stores. Purchase only exterior, incandescent floodlights designated for outdoor use. These lamps come in a wide variety of sizes and wattages for almost any need. Incandescent lights tend to throw a wide-angle beam, but reflectors in some lamp designs can increase brightness and make the beam easier to focus. Narrow-beam lamps are useful for lighting side passages next to your home or to light other tight areas. A hardware store should be able to help you find narrow-beam or other specialty lamps to suit your needs. Floodlights should sit high, preferably around or above the recommended minimum mounting height of eight feet. Cast floodlight beams at a downward angle across the desired area. This throws the bright central portion of the beam on your property and reduces spill-over light into adjacent units or neighboring homes.

▶ HID, or high-intensity discharge lights are extremely bright, efficient, and long-lasting. These units, excellent for lighting broad areas, do require a specialized light fixture and a ballast. Note that most HID lamps require warm up time, sometimes several minutes, so aren't ideal for any application where instant illumination is important.

▶ Tungsten-Halogen lights have a long life and are brighter per watt than incandescent bulbs. Small Tungsten bulbs work well for recessed lighting in eves to provide lighting over exterior doors or around the home exterior.

▶ Low voltage, underground-wired lighting systems save energy and are useful for lighting gardens and dark areas around landscaping. The fixtures usually anchor in the ground, and have a variety of applications, from lighting pathways for safety to lighting fences or privacy walls for security. Although usually not as bright as other lighting types, a well designed, low-voltage system alone can sufficiently illuminate a yard or an area to prevent anyone from hiding there unseen. Hiring an installer for this type of work is not expensive, although do-it-yourself kits are widely available in garden centers. Note that these projects do require some electrical know-how as well as knowledge of your local codes. Household voltage must be stepped down via a transformer from 120VAC to, typically, 12 volts direct current. In some locations, underground wiring codes require partial or full conduit, fixtures and lines must be grounded or protected by ground fault interrupters (GFIs), and lines must be buried between 18" and 24" deep. Local code may require a permit depending on where you are digging, and you'll certainly need to know were any gas or other lines run on your property. If you do tackle this project yourself, follow all local codes, electrical safety measures, and be sure your transformer(s) are adequate to handle the lamps and fixtures you intend to run from it.

CHAPTER 12
Looking Lived In

Although bold, armed home intrusions dominate the news, the majority of burglars avoid encounters with homeowners or residents. The more it appears that your residence is occupied, the less likely that it becomes a target. A few common sense measures can make a big difference in how your home appears to a would-be burglar.

Reaching Out: Community Security

The behavior of those who live near and around you greatly affects home and personal security. Perhaps you live in an apartment complex where people routinely move in and out. Would any of your neighbors give a second glance if a stranger were hauling your property out of your apartment into an awaiting truck? If you live in a single-family home, do you know the neighbors in the homes adjacent to your property? Do you live in a small town where your business is everyone's business?

If you answered "no" to all the questions in the previous paragraph, you're not alone. People relocate more than in previous generations, change jobs more often, and have a host of technical devices that distract and capture their attention. You may be "wired in" to the world, yet completely, socially disconnected from the community in which you live. You can't blame the situation entirely on city size; some neighborhoods in Manhattan are as socially connected and protective as are some small towns.

You need connections with your neighbors to help protect your home, and your neighbors need you for the same reason. If you're out of town, for example, a friendly neighbor can help with daily routines such as newspaper collection that, if left undone, can signal to a thief that no one is home.

Many feel intimidated or anxious about engaging or getting acquainted with neighbors. It's hard for some to take the first step, to simply say hello, to introduce themselves or start a conversation. If you're a gregarious type who makes friends easily, you may know several neighbors already. If you are shy and live in an area where residents act distrustful, connecting with your neighbors can seem more difficult. Try small and sustained efforts to recognize, greet and, hopefully, get to know your neighbors. The innate, human social nature is on your side.

Neighborhood organizations, social events or gatherings are excellent places to initiate contact. One organization establishes social contact for the specific purpose of discouraging and preventing crime.

Neighborhood Watch Programs

The National Sheriff's Neighborhood Watch Program offers assistance in connecting with neighbors. You've probably heard of this initiative, as it has been around for close to fifty years, and has a strong track record of linking neighbors and law enforcement in an effort to reduce crime. The program has resources and tool-kits that explain how to organize Neighborhood Watch programs – and can help you break the ice with your neighbors by providing an organized, purposeful forum for meeting.

First, find out if there is an existing neighborhood watch program in your area and participate. If no such program exists for your street or neighborhood, contact your local police and ask if a law enforcement liaison will assist you in starting one.

Neighborhood Watch Program Website: http://www.usaonwatch.org/Resources/ResourceCenter.php

Neighborhood Watch Mailing Address: National Sheriffs' Association

1450 Duke Street, Alexandria, Virginia 22314-3490

Looking Lived-in: Mail, Vehicles and More

If you leave home for more than a day or two, your absence grows more apparent with each passing day - unless you've taken preventative steps. Neighbors or trusted friends play a critical role in maintaining the illusion that your residence is occupied.

Items for Neighbors or Friends

> ▶ Park a vehicle, or ask a neighbor to park a vehicle, in front of your house or in your driveway while you are away. Placing your vehicles in a garage may secure the cars, but removes a major indicator that someone might be home.

> ▶ If your trash collection service involves placing a bin or dumpster out-side the door or at curb side, ask a neighbor or friend to use your dumpster occasionally and to place it out on the appropriate day. Make sure they'll remove the bin following trash collection. A receptacle sitting on the curb days after others in the neighborhood have retrieved their bins is a sign of an unoccupied home.

> ▶ Ask a neighbor to collect mail, newspapers, door-handle sales pieces, and other flyers. Placing a temporary stop on mail delivery at the post of-fice is helpful, but your property still may accumulate items or packages delivered by other carriers.

Items for You

> ▶   A neglected lawn is a sign that homeowners may be on vacation. Make certain you arrange in advance to have your lawn trimmed in a timely fashion while you are absent. Arrange for snow removal as needed.

> ▶   Establish consistent home appearance. Close blinds and curtains in unoccupied rooms and leave at least one light on at night. Mirror this appearance when you travel. The more consistent your home appears, the more difficult it will be to determine whether you are home or away.

> ▶   Before you leave for business or vacation travel, check the appearance of your home from the street. Have you "shut the house down" in any way that changes the appearance of the residence compared to when you are home? If you rarely close some blinds when you are in the home, leave them partially open when away.

> ▶   Some sounds signal occupancy as clearly as visual cues. Turn down phone ringers and answering machines

> ▶   Review the 'appearance of occupancy' security checklist items in Chapter 3.

These active steps remove the most obvious cues that you are not at home. Additional measures make it even harder to discern if your residence is occupied or not.

Interior Lighting and Sound

Light timers

Although "leaving a light on" when you are away from home is better than leaving the lights off, inexpensive and more active solutions are available. A simple electric timer that allows multiple on-off times for lights costs under $10. Use at least two of these when you are away from home, with one timed light located in a bathroom, the one room that could plausibly occupied anytime, day or night. Set lights to turn on and off at varying intervals, but make sure that at least one light remains on at all times. Some security timers on the market turn lights on and off at random intervals ranging from a few minutes to a little over half-an-hour. Use two or three of these timers connected to lamps in different parts of the home, and your residence will appear active and occupied. These designed-for-security devices typically offer two settings: a standard mode that allows the light to be used normally, and a security mode that activates the random timer.

Televisions / radios

Thieves sometimes ring doorbells or knock, prepared to pose as a salesperson or someone who is lost if an occupant answers. Leave a television or radio on, loud enough to be heard from outside your entry door, and you create at least some doubt about whether you are home or not. People watch television at virtually any time of day or night, and you might well be inside, perhaps asleep or wearing head-phones, and unable hear the door over the noise of the television The fact that you *just might* be home is sufficient to ward off some intruders. The same timers used for random lighting work for audio devices such as radio or television sets. Set timers to turn on sound-producing devices in different rooms of the home at varying times.

You can take this approach a step further with "barking dog" or other doorbell alarms. These systems play a looped tape of a large, barking dog should someone ring the bell or, with some systems, when windows or doors are disturbed or vibrate. Some systems use multiple speakers. If the bell is sounded twice, the barks (often a different series of barks) will be routed to the second speaker, creating the impression that a very real dog has moved within the home. Most intruders prefer to avoid dogs, and this can be a useful, supplemental security measure.

CHAPTER 13
Protecting Valuables

Safety Deposit Boxes vs. Home Safes

Most thieves are out to steal high value items that are easily carried and concealed. Jewelry and watches are particularly attractive and are easy to pawn or fence. Guns are extremely easy to sell on the black market to those who cannot purchase weapons legally. Laptops, DVD and BlueRay® players, and other small electronic devices (smart phones, video cameras) are all prime targets for theft.

Thieves won't treat your home with respect. In an effort to find valuable items, they'll toss about, break or otherwise damage personal keepsakes, photographs, or documents. It's not practical to lock up everything you own of value, but certain items do merit the security of a safety deposit box or a high-quality home safe.

If you don't already have one, rent a safety deposit box at your local bank. While a home safe reduces the risk of theft, a safety deposit box all but guarantees security. With enough time, even a highly tamper resistant home safe can be defeated, and there's always the possibility that you could be forced to open a home safe. A safety deposit box is off-premises and offers protection systems that can't be matched in the home. This is the best place to store very important documents that you do not need to access regularly. In the event of theft, fire, or flood at your home, you will still have access to these important papers and materials should you need them.

Items to keep in a *safety deposit box:*

- Marriage, divorce, birth, and death records
- Your personal will
- Stock certificates, bond certificates, treasury notes, and savings bonds
- Deeds and titles to land, vehicles, or other property
- Records of significant business transactions
- Photographs, video, and an inventory of your home property
- Valuable jewelry, coins, or other expensive items not routinely used

Items to keep in a safety deposit box *or* home safe:

- Professional licenses or certificates
- Essential medical and dental records
- Passports or visas
- Military records
- Computer Data Backups
- Important or expensive computer software
- Valuable coins, jewelry, and expensive watches
- Homeowners and auto insurance policies
- Your Social Security Card
- Military records
- Important receipts
- Employment contracts
- 401K and/or Pension Plan documents

Types of Home Safes

A quality home safe stores valuables out of sight, and presents a difficult, time-consuming obstacle to the average burglar. Home safes may not keep intruders out of your home, but they may reduce the extent of your property loss.

Home safes commonly are either wall mounted, floor mounted, or in-floor designs. Gun safes are purpose-specific safes designed to secure firearms. Gun safes vary enormously in size and design, and some models may serve well as general home safes. Note, though, that larger gun safes can't easily be concealed.

Wall Mounted Safes

Wall mounted safes fit into the wall spaces between studs. In order for the safe door to sit flush with the wall for easy concealment, the depth of the safe is limited to the thickness of the wall. Typically, these safes have about 3 ½ inches of depth, useful for storing small items or paperwork, but insufficient for larger or odd-sized valuables. Note that a 3 ½-inch deep wall safe offers minimal fire protection. Although highly fire-resistant wall safes are available, they typically must be much deeper than 3 ½ inches in order to accommodate fire-insulating material. Most homes lack walls thick enough to accept highly fire-resistant wall safes. On the positive side, wall safes readily hide behind paintings or other wall hangings, and may therefore be situated in any room. Wall safes mounted at chest or eye level allow you to view the contents without bending or stooping. Finally, the mounting height of wall safes offers some protection against water damage if lower levels of the home should flood. If you are comfortable cutting and repairing drywall, you can save money by installing a 3 1/2 inch deep wall safe yourself. Be sure to follow the manufacturer's mounting instructions for the specific safe you purchase.

Floor Mounted Safes

Floor mounted safes rest on the floor either against a wall or in a corner - they are not recessed into the floor structure. The back of a closet or other concealed area is a common location. Floor mounted safes come in a broad range of sizes and shapes. Protection grades vary, and safes may be theft resistant, fire resistant or both. Floor safes may claim to be waterproof or flood resistant, but it's wise to keep very important papers in a safety deposit box or, at minimum, seal important papers or documents in watertight bags or containers before placing them in a floor safe. Floor safes have a fire resistance advantage over wall safes as hot, rising air leaves the floor the coolest spot in the residence in the event of a fire. Floor safes anchor to floor joists, wall studs or to concrete surfaces or foundations) with sturdy bolts or screws. The heads of these bolts or screws are accessed only from inside the open safe.   Floor safes may be placed and anchored on both ground or second story floors. It's not difficult to install a floor safe if you plan to anchor it to a wall stud or floor joist.   You need only an electric drill, a few hand tools and the directions for installing the model of safe you own.

Anchoring to concrete walls or foundation flooring is the strongest way to secure a floor safe. Anchoring to concrete isn't terribly difficult, but you may need to own or rent a hammer drill in order to pre-drill anchor holes in foundation flooring or concrete surfaces. That said, it's inexpensive to hire a professional locksmith to install a floor safe for you, regardless of the anchoring material. A professional can often complete the job in less than an hour, and this may cost you less than if you rent gear such as a hammer drill and do it yourself. In fact, it can cost you a *lot less* if you don't know what you're doing and cause serious damage to your foundation or concrete surfaces.

In-Floor Safes

In-floor safes are recessed into the ground (or floor) and reside completely below the floor surface. The door is accessed and opened from the top. These safes require cutting through the floor or foundation and digging out an opening to accommodate the safe. The safe lowers into the pre-dug and leveled opening, and concrete is poured to firmly anchor the safe in place. An in floor safe isn't going anywhere; if a thief can't pick the lock, they're probably out of luck. Should you ever build your own home, consider having a sizable in-floor safe installed at the time the foundation is poured. You'll have a large, very solidly anchored safe, and you'll add resale value to your home.

Unless you're experienced or you do this sort of work for a living, it's not recommend that you cut large holes in your concrete floor. Qualified locksmiths and safe installers understand placement (i.e., floor safes placed in corners are more difficult for thieves), have appropriate tools, and can handle this job quickly and correctly for you. It's possible, depending on the design of your home, to install an in-floor safe on a second story floor or on a floor above a basement. These installations bypass the extra degree of security offered by a recessed concrete setting, as the safe must be anchored to wood floor joists or wall studs.

In-floor safes anchored in concrete offer strong theft security, and some models are rated for fire resistance. A safe buried in a concrete basement floor offers inherent fire resistance, but is also vulnerable to flooding. Some in-floor safes claim to be water proof, but it's not worth risking your most valuable possessions by testing such a safe if you live in an area with the potential for prolonged, standing water as a result of flooding. Use a safety deposit box for irreplaceable documents or items.

Regardless of type, your safe should have a lock that carries an approval rating from Underwriters Laboratory (UL). Underwriters Laboratory also rates safes for fire resistance. UL fire-rates safes in two ways. First, UL rates safes based on how long the safe resists fire temperatures, and is expressed in time. Most fire resistant safes are rated from thirty minutes up to four hours for top-end safes. Second, the UL rating may also classify the fire resistance of a safe based on the materials it capably protects:

Class 350: Papers, currencies, and documents

Class 150: Photographic film and magnetic tape

Class 125: Computer floppy disks

If you remain in doubt about what type of safe you need or how to anchor it, contact a locksmith or a safe installation company for assistance.

Simple Panic or Safe Room Setup

Property loss is insignificant compared to the risk of serious bodily injury or death at the hands of an intruder. Not all criminals flee if they hear a noise or encounter a home occupant. Drug addicts, the habitually violent, those with mental disorders or that simply lack any compassion or regard for human life - these types may seek confrontation rather than avoid it. The most frightening scenarios involve a violent intruder or intruders who intend to harm you or family members. Short of active self defense with or without a firearm or the presence of a trained security dog (see Chapter 16), few passive measures are available to protect personal safety once an intruder is in the home.

The term "safe room" has several meanings. Disaster management agencies such as FEMA refer to safe rooms to describe tornado or hurricane resistant rooms within a residence or commercial building. Safe rooms or "panic rooms" also describe rooms designed to protect residents from intruders long enough to summon police and for police to arrive. Safe rooms are effective only if there is sufficient warning and time for residents to retreat to and secure the safe room.

Safe rooms have long been in use by the rich and powerful or by those with danger-ous, personal or political enemies. Some safe rooms feature reinforced concrete walls and thick steel doors with specialized locks, secure communication to the out-side world, and other survival equipment. A safe room can have as many protective features as you have money to spend.

You probably can't afford to duplicate the kind of safe rooms sometimes depicted in movies, but you can create a space that buys additional time to trigger an alarm system or to summon the police. A room, bathroom, basement or closet with a single entrance and with few or no windows is the best selection. If you must create a safe room that has windows, install window security screens or grates. In addition to window safety, reinforce the entrance in as many of the following ways as pos-sible:

▶ Replace the existing interior door with a solid steel door.

▶ Use steel doorjamb reinforcements or a full steel door frame.

▶ Hang the door with the hinge pins inside the room or use concealed or non-removable hinge-pins.

▶ Install at least one, high-security dead bolt lock and secure the strike plate with long security screws

▶ Place an alarm panel, panic button or, at minimum, a cell phone in the safe room.

▶ Ensure the room has a switched light, a working flashlight, and ad-equate ventilation.

These measures create a very basic safe room. If you want reinforced walls or other specialized solutions, contact a security contractor to review your options.

Property Identification

Rarely do victims recover stolen property. Watches, laptops, and other electronics are common, so pawnshops or police often can't definitively tie these items to a crime. The following measures do not prevent theft, but do increase the odds that your property may be recovered.

Recording Keeping

Many valuable items have a unique serial number (i.e., guns, guitars, cameras, most electronics). Write serial numbers down along with the item information and store this information away from the home. One efficient method is to take a photograph of valuable items and write the serial numbers, makes, and models on the back. Alternatively, annotate digital photographs with the same information and store on a removable, digital storage device. Another method is to create a videotape inventory of your home. Walk through every room, taking clear, still video of all valuable items. Read the serial numbers and other information aloud (be sure you are recording audio as well as video). Regardless of method, store one copy of the paper, photo, or videotape in a safety deposit box.

Marking Property

Mark electronic equipment, watches and other valuables with an engraver's tool. Use symbols, numbers or words that identify the items as your own. Document your chosen i.d. method in your property records. Don't use your Social Security number or other sensitive information – there's no need to assist with identity theft. If you don't have access to an engraver's tool, you can buy a security-grade, waterproof, invisible ink marker from a home security supplier or most locksmiths.

Interior Visibility

It's not realistic or desirable to keep shades and blinds closed at all times. It's also unwise to unnecessarily display valuables to the outside world. Take the following precautions to reduce the visibility of the interior of your home from outside.

Basic Precautions

Don't routinely leave valuables anywhere they are visible to someone legitimately approaching your home via a sidewalk, porch or entryway. Remember that thieves may convincingly pose as salespersons or service personnel while they "case" your residence. Don't allow any unknown or unexpected visitors inside the home or into any area where they have a clear view of your home interior.

Drapes and Shades

Use window treatments that, when closed, fully obscure or hide your home interior. Use shades, drapes or blinds on all French doors, sliding glass doors and large windows. Venetian or slatted style blinds often may be partially opened to allow light into the home without permitting a good view of the interior. Some semi-sheer drapes or hangings allow a great deal of light into the room but are opaque from outside. Note that these same hangings may offer a transparent view into the home at night when the primary light source is inside the home.

Reflective window films

You may wish to leave blinds or shades open on French doors, patio doors or large picture windows during the day. These portals offer an inviting view of your belongings to potential thieves, and make it much easier to determine whether or not you are home. There are solutions. Several companies manufacture window films that act as a one-way mirror. In daylight, these films appear as an opaque surface when viewed from the outside, but are nearly transparent when viewed from the interior of the home.   However, many of these films produce the opposite effect at night, and allow potential intruders a clear view of the interior. Reflective films aren't stand-alone solutions; supplementary blinds and shades must be in place for night-time privacy. If you do plan on using window films in your residence, consider break resistant privacy films to further increase window security.

CHAPTER 14
The Internet and Home Security

When you hear the term digital security, you probably first think about identity theft, credit card fraud, or the damages caused by computer viruses. The physical security of your home or the possibility of burglary likely aren't the first digital dangers that come to mind.

You are, however, probably are aware of the many concerns created by the growth of digital, online, and mobile communications, particularly if you have children. The explosion of social media and mobile applications is stunning. People are connecting, reconnecting and communicating in new ways that, unfortunately, they don't always fully understand. One result of all this digital technology is unprecedented public access to what was previously private, or reasonably private, information. Unfortunately, there are those who will use such information in ways that directly threaten your personal and property security.

Web Insecurity

Children are no longer the only family members that may lack prudence in the digital world as it pertains to home security. A quick check of Facebook™, MySpace™, or any of the other "social sharing" applications provide astonishing insight into the lives of people you don't know. Many otherwise responsible adults post vacation photos and updates while they are still away from home. They advertise, on a global level, that their home is likely vacant and vulnerable. Chat rooms, instant messaging and e-mail are "old school", online avenues for criminals to gather information and to identify targets or victims. The evolving world of digital communication creates new avenues for burglars, sexual predators, and other criminals to exploit almost daily.

You likely use the internet for many purposes, from booking travel and shopping to online banking. Most of the well-known and reputable services are reasonably safe - at least with regard to home security, and avoiding the internet isn't the point. You must understand your role and your limitations in protecting digital security.

Your Life on the Web - Like it or Not

Even if you don't own a computer, you'd likely be shocked by the amount of your personal information that can be found or bought online in a matter of seconds. An inexpensive background search provides your current address, previous addresses, criminal records and a host of related information. Googlemaps™ currently allows anyone in the world to see a virtual "drive by view" of homes or apartments in many cities and towns.   A number of governments are investigating if such technology constitutes an illegal invasion of privacy but, for today, the technology is freely available to almost anyone with a laptop and an internet connection. It's bad enough that strangers can effortlessly learn so much about you. Don't augment the problem by misuse of social networks, chat, dating services, instant messaging and other sharing applications. Opportunistic thieves may note someone who has communicated work hours, household habits, when they're out of town, or other information useful to thieves. The thieves may be able to find out where the home is and attempt to take advantage of their knowledge. It's equally important to understand that "delete" functions don't necessarily destroy online data or information. Web information is often "cached," or stored in an effort to improve the efficiency of the web. Data deleted months, sometimes years earlier, may turn up in search engine results or elsewhere. Your life is on the web, sometimes irrevocably so, whether you like it or not.

Personal Profiles

Social media services, online dating applications, job networking sites - most of these require users have some sort of personal profile. If you're seeking to connect or reconnect with friends, your name alone is sufficient for people you know to find you. Share more private information, such as phone numbers, your living status, or your work hours only through direct e-mail or other channels -- and only with individuals you trust. Fortunately, unless you are or have been the victim of a personal stalker, telling the world where you went to high school or college, about your favorite band, your favorite food, or your favorite charity generally doesn't pose an immediate threat to the security of your home. Before you post public information, ask yourself this:

Does the information *in any way* help a stranger determine if you live alone or when you are at home or not? If the answer is yes, don't post it. If such information is required, seek another service. Remember, whether or not your address is posted is irrelevant. With a name and an approximate age, your current residence may return on background search reports widely available to the general public. Lest you think that use of such report services will lead police to the criminal, think again. Criminals can access such reports using stolen credit cards and false identities.

Privacy Settings

The web is a powerful, productive tool, a tool that's become an essential part of daily life. However, information and data in digital form is often not nearly as secure as you may believe. Most of the major interactive applications are aware of security issues and work diligently to enhance privacy controls and settings, but they are far from perfect. Social media applications remain works in progress and *do not* provide bullet-proof privacy controls. Privacy controls aren't clear or easy to find on all applications, and the user may simply fail to employ them, or to understand and employ them correctly. Many privacy controls are routinely changed or upgraded as the operators of these platforms adjust to ever-changing, perceived or real security threats. Government regulators are far behind the curve, and are just beginning to address some of the security concerns presented by new web platforms. It's *up to users* to understand what privacy controls are available, what they claim to do - and what they *really* do. Few have time to experiment and tinker; it's wise to set any application privacy controls as high as possible. Even that is insufficient: digital privacy, at least today, is a contradiction in terms. There is tremendous traffic in information sales and exchange, and the laws are well behind the technologies. Circumvent the issue altogether. Even if it crimps your personal style, offer little or no personal information in public or even supposedly private, online forums.

Posting Photos Online

Many understand that posting photos of your vacation *while you are on vacation* is one of the most glaring, digital security errors you can make. You simply publicize that you are out of town and away from home. Remember, it's not difficult for anyone to find out *where* you live. If you simply can't wait to show images or tell the details of your trip, share only via direct e-mail or make a phone call.

Tragically, property is not the only criminal, digital target. Sexual predators may focus on your home for another, more sinister reason. Women and children are the most common targets - and they are increasingly targeted and victimized in their own homes.

For singles, this is problematic. Online dating has moved into the mainstream and is embraced by many attractive, successful singles who don't wish to find romance at the office or in bars. The legitimate reason and desire to post flattering pictures is understandable. Most online dating services offer a great deal of advice and information on appropriate security precautions for online dating, and you should thoroughly read and heed such advice. As obvious as it may sound, don't post photographs that show off expensive property or that identify where your live.

Parents and grandparents are often proud of youngsters in the family. You may be inclined to "show the world" your attractive son, grandson, daughter or granddaughter. Unlike online dating, there is no compelling argument that this is necessary. It's best to electronically share photos of family or children in direct e-mail. If you must post them on a sharing site, review the security options, and grant access only those you implicitly trust. Just know those photos are now in cyber-space.

Children and the Web

Pedophilia is an immense problem, and too many cases involve abduction of children from near or within their own homes. These cases make a compelling argument for use of many of the home security measures discussed in this book. However, these measures are compromised if a child is compliant, or trusts the perpetrator and provides them with information that grants them entrance into the home.

Banning or limiting web use and prohibiting chat site or social network use may work for children up to a certain age, and even for some very obedient teens. Others, overcome by curiosity or peer pressure, will experiment. Children today have never known a world without instantaneous global connectivity. It's naive to believe that kids and, particularly, teens, won't want to be a part of it - or that they will diligently follow parental rules any better than did previous generations.

It's improbable that you can constantly, personally monitor computer or gaming system use (gaming systems, too, now often involve large, interactive communities). You may have some success restricting PC use through parental-control software, but this is generally effective only for very young children. Don't underestimate the technical savvy of youth; it is hard to prevent a determined teenager from working around software controls designed to restrict computer use. Furthermore, computers are ubiquitous. It's even harder to prevent your child from accessing computers outside the home that have no usage restrictions.

Involve yourself in your child's online activities. If you allow them to use social media, help them set up appropriate profiles and to set privacy settings to the highest levels possible.

Teach your children about online sharing boundaries -- just as they have long been taught to beware of strangers. Teach them of the warning signs that an online contact may not be well intended:

Strive to help your children:

> ▶ Be very wary of people that they have never met in person who contact them. E-mail, instant messages or posts to social media pages by strangers should be brought to the attention of parents or, at minimum, deleted.

> ▶ Understand that, online, it's very easy to pretend to be someone you are not. Explain how easy it is to create a profile or account on a popular service using a false name, identity, age, gender, etc. Help your children understand that they must only communicate with those they know in person.

> ▶ Distrust online flattery or empathy. Predators know that low self esteem often accompanies adolescence. They'll often attempt to befriend youngsters by telling them how attractive, special, or smart they are, or that they have a special understanding of how they feel and what they are experiencing. Do your best to help you kids understand that flattery and empathy are often used to manipulate and entice online - just as they are in the offline world.

> ▶ Understand information boundaries, just as they are taught to understand "touching" boundaries on their own bodies. For home security purposes, it's critical that information concerning what goes on in the home

or with the family schedule is considered completely private. If anyone asks who lives in the home, who works and when, who goes to school and where or any information at all about the in-home specifics should immediately be brought to the attention of parents.

▶   Realize that predators may be very intelligent and very patient. Warn children that private topics can be broached in a way that may seem very innocent. Make sure they understand that "knowing" someone for a long time online is meaningless. Information boundaries must be guarded online. Always.

You know your children best. Use the methods and styles that work for your family, but don't ignore this aspect of home security. Alarms, gates, locks, lighting - none of them are of help if a criminal is allowed into the home by a family member, or if a family member essentially helps "case" the home for the would-be perpetrator.

CHAPTER 15
Outside The Home

Burglars may target your home before they even know where it is. How? They need only to target *you* with the knowledge that sooner or later, you'll lead them to your residence. Your behavior outside the home influences the likelihood of such secondary targeting. Flashy jewelry, expensive watches or similar displays of wealth certainly attract the attention of criminals, but less motivation is often sufficient. It's not uncommon for criminals to note a victim carrying a simple laptop computer, and to discretely follow them home or to another location where robbery or theft is easy. Even if you don't dress expensively, wear jewelry or own a laptop, some behaviors increase risk. Simple precautions are in order.

Key Security Away from Home

If you valet park or use a car wash or other service that requires your keys, be sure your key ring allows you detach all keys but those needed to operate the vehicle. An opportunist can make an impression of house keys quickly and easily. This is another example of how and why unforced entry accounts for almost a third of burglaries. Don't invest in expensive security hardware only to help thieves circumvent it.

Verbal Advertising

Don't discuss your valuable possessions with strangers or where strangers might overhear. Recently, a man in a bar bragged to a friend about his collection of rare baseball memorabilia. Two days later, he lost his collection in an aggravated home invasion. Fortunately, police caught the robber, a bar patron who had over-heard the conversation and followed the man home. The criminal even spent a few days determining that the home was equipped with solid security systems and that he'd be better off using swift confrontation and threat of force. Only a small portion of the valued collection was recovered.

Windows of Opportunity

Beware of astonishingly quick smash-and-grabs, even in your own driveway. Many people use laptops and mobile devices in coffee shops, bookstores and other public places. Example: A businessman used his laptop in a restaurant and then "concealed" it in the back of his SUV and headed home. Just seconds after he parked in the driveway and entered his home, he heard a loud crash followed by the sound of a vehicle racing away. When he investigated, he found the rear SUV window smashed and the laptop gone. Based on the speed of the theft, police concluded the thief or thieves observed the man at the restaurant, noted where he placed the laptop, and followed him home. Furthermore, police noted this was not an unusual practice. Anytime you display something valuable in public, take note of your surroundings and remove the valuable(s) from your vehicle at the earliest opportunity. If your vehicle has a trunk or other lockable compartment, secure all valuables within.

Arriving Home

If you implement most of the security measures described in this book, and if you consistently arm a monitored alarm system, it's far less likely you'll walk in on a burglary in progress. However, no security system is foolproof and there's always the possibility that you might forget to arm your alarm system. You may come home to find signs that an intrusion has taken place. The thief usually has gone, along with many of your belongings. Don't rely on it. There's a chance an intruder is inside your home.

If you see *anything* unusual when you return home, such as an open door or a broken window, do not enter the home - whether your alarm has triggered or not. Leave the premises, preferably in your vehicle, and call the police. Do not attempt to investigate yourself, even if you are armed. This is no time for heroics. You may face an experienced thief who is fully prepared to use violence, or a highly strung, unpredictable drug addict who is simply trying to steal enough to support a habit. Don't fool yourself by thinking you have the upper hand because you have "surprised" the thief. They may have heard you arriving and may be hiding or waiting in a spot that provides them with good cover. There may be more than one intruder in or around the home.

Even if you do catch a lone thief by surprise, adrenaline and desperation may cause them to react with violence. Adrenaline will course through your body, too, producing instant, physiological symptoms. You'll be tense and your heart rate will soar resulting in significantly impaired fine motor skills.

In any of the above scenarios, you'll have needlessly placed yourself in an extremely dangerous position. There is simply no sensible reason to risk injury or death by seeking confrontation with an intruder. Leave and dial for emergency help.

CHAPTER 16
Dogs and Firearms

Dogs and firearms occupy a short and separate section of this book for a specific reason. Not everyone wants to have, can have, or should have a dog, and the same is even more true of guns. *Moreover, each of these topics merit a full book (or books) to completely cover all considerations. A comprehensive discussion of these topics is beyond the scope of this work.* However, if you want the security benefits of a guard dog or feel that a self-defense weapon (firearm or otherwise) is right for you, information is your ally. This chapter offers an overview of the numerous issues involved with both dog and gun ownership, and points out that security experts often disagree on these subjects. Perform substantial, additional research before you act.

Security Dogs: Considerations and Concerns

Dogs often make an excellent addition to the security of your home and provide an active element that mechanical or electronic security devices can't replicate. The very presence of a dog in a residence may be enough to dissuade some potential intruders, although stories, and even videos, exist showing thieves in action, petting and playing with the victim's "security" dog.   Understand that simply owning a pet dog does not mean they'll make an effective security animal. Training is essential, but also does not guarantee predictable animal behavior under highly unusual circumstances. Dogs are often highly effective, but as a category do not represent an insurmountable defense against crime. Owning a dog is no excuse for failing to exercise other, simple security precautions as outlined in preceding chapters.

If you are not an experienced dog owner, you may underestimate the personal responsibilities, including day-to-day feeding, taking care of bodily needs, veterinary care and costs, arranging for pet housing when you are out of town, and more. Some breeds require significant exercise that may not be realistic in some urban settings. Other breeds may not tolerate frequent or unfamiliar visitors to the home. Some breeds are excellent with children and other household pets, some breeds are not. The attributes of various breeds, and whether or not those attributes fit into your living space and lifestyle must be determined beforehand. Members of your family may be uncomfortable with dogs, or my have significant pet allergies that should be uncovered *before* you commit to animal ownership. Don't lose sight of the fact that dog ownership carries moral and legal obligations - both for care of the animal and for the animal's actions, and that legal considerations may vary from state to state.

Your first inclination may be to obtain a large breed dog, or a breed often recommended for home security (i.e., Bull Mastiff, Doberman Pinscher, German Shepherd). While these dogs may make an excellent addition to the household – and serve as a strong deterrent to intruders -- a well-trained small dog also can be useful. For many intruders, the threat of detection is reason enough to flee the premises. A small dog that barks incessantly when a stranger approaches may be sufficient to warn anyone inside the home and often will send a would-be thief looking for a quieter target.

After you have settled on a breed, consider practical details, such as where the dog will spend most of its time. If a dog is to be outdoors for part of the day, you need a securely fenced yard or other means to prevent it from leaving the property. If the dog is a potential threat to non-family members, a "beware of dog" sign is essential to warn legitimate workers or visitors of the danger. Check your local laws or consult with an attorney to understand your criminal and civil liability. Also, be aware that an outdoors-only dog is unable to do much except bark in the event an intruder enters or confronts you inside the home.

Firearms, the Law, and You

Camps are split on the efficacy of firearms for home protection, with some claiming the danger of accident outweighs the benefits, to those who vow that competent and safe handling negate these dangers. In spite of the statistical dangers of accident, there is also merit to the saying that you may never need a gun, but if you do, you'll need it badly. The saying also highlights the fact that guns will not help achieve the objective of *making your home a less attractive crime target*. Guns are primarily used to halt or change the outcome of a crime or an attempted crime through the threat or use of deadly force.

There are legal, moral, and personal considerations to firearm possession and potential use. Gun ownership is an individual matter, and only you can weigh risks and benefits against your values, abilities, and living situation. If you own or are considering purchase of a firearm, *you are obligated* to understand all legal issues that may apply. You must be familiar with local, state, and federal laws regarding firearms and use of deadly force, and be aware that violations can result in incarceration. Realize, too, that even fully lawful use of deadly force usually won't prevent civil action.

Frequently regulated areas include:

- ▶ Who can own a gun. Some people can't own or purchase guns legally (those with prior convictions for various classes of felonies or misdemeanors, depending on state law, for example).

- ▶ Gun sales or transfer. The transfer or sale of a gun may require registration, a background check, or other procedures.

- ▶ Concealed weapon carriage. As of this writing, in states such as Vermont, no permit is required for a legal gun owner to carry a concealed

weapon. States increasingly allow and issue permits or licenses for concealed weapons carriage, but the applicable laws and regulations vary.
Other states continue ban carriage outright. The laws in some states may
prohibit carrying an unloaded gun, concealed or otherwise, outside your
residence except for transport to and from a shooting range. Penalties for
violations can be stiff, and laws don't follow you from state-to-state. Concealed carriage permits, which may or may not be reciprocally recognized
between any two, given states, don't exempt you. When you cross state
lines, you are subject to *all* firearms regulations of the state you are entering.

▶   Deadly force. As with concealed weapons, state law varies greatly on
the use of deadly force. Your well-intended self-defense efforts could result
in a murder or manslaughter charge if the circumstances aren't within local,
legal definitions.

▶   Gun Security. In many states, leaving an unsecured firearm within
access of a minor is a serious offense. A violation can result in significant
fines or incarceration, particularly in the event a minor accesses the gun
and injures someone. Legally required security measures, and even the
definition of a "minor" varies state to state.

If you are not comfortable with firearms or if you do not know how to shoot properly,
consult with a qualified gun safety instructor *before purchasing or firing* a weapon.
These professionals can help you select an appropriate weapon and can provide
safety and marksmanship training. Many local gun shops or shooting ranges employ
a qualified firearms instructor or can recommend one.

There is much debate over the "best" personal or home defense weapon. Some
advocate foregoing space-saving convenience and concealable qualities for a 12

gauge shotgun loaded with 00-buck shot for unrivalled stopping power. Others recommend a handgun loaded with "safety" ammunition that will penetrate flesh, but will not pass through walls - a serious consideration for the safety of other innocent people in your home or apartment, and a notable drawback to 12 gauge shotguns loaded with 00-buck shot. Some even argue that only a semi-automatic, military-style rifle (known widely as assault rifles, although that term is a misnomer) is adequate given reports that some intruders have been apprehended wearing body armor. Firearm size, recoil or "kick," and a host of other factors must be weighed based on the size, strength, skill, needs and preferences of the owner.

Are you legally able and willing to have a loaded weapon in your home that is quickly accessible? An unloaded gun, or a gun that must be retrieved from a safe or locked drawer might cost precious seconds that change the outcome of a home intrusion - yet such measures may be legally required if children are present. Do you need a high capacity firearm, or is a six-shot revolver sufficient? What caliber and/or ammunition loads will meet your self defense needs? How often will you be able to practice with your firearm? If you're not highly familiar and adept with a firearm in the relative safety of a firing range, it's unrealistic to expect you'll be able to mount an effective defense under the extreme stress of a crime situation. Will you have the nerve to use deadly force if necessary? Will you have the presence of mind to consider what is beyond your target and make a split-second determination if firing might endanger a family member or another innocent person? Do you take prescription medications or other drugs that may impair your judgment?

It's equally important to understand that owning a firearm does not obligate you to defend your home with lethal force. It's not recommended that an amateur, even if armed, attempt to seek out and confront intruders. A plan for where family members will seek safety and how police will be contacted is important, but such plans can fail due to stress, chaos, or the fact that things simply didn't happen as the plan envisioned. Firearms offer no hard guarantee that you will be able to protect your family, property, or yourself. Whether you choose to arm yourself or not, it's best if you implement other effective, home security measures that deter, prevent, or warn that a crime is taking or about to take place.

This book points out *just a few* of the questions and considerations surrounding firearms and deadly force for home protection. Education, professional consultation and hands-on training are mandatory if you are considering a personal firearm.

You will quickly find that even qualified, expert opinions on the subject vary widely. Even after you've done your homework, you'll face some decisions that fully depend on your personal judgement, needs, and living circumstances. There's certainly no shame should you decide that firearms aren't right or safe for you.

Lastly, firearms, like dogs, are not a substitute for due consideration to all the other passive security items offered in this book and to the importance of remaining vigilant.

Final Thoughts

It is worth restating that security efforts are additive. For the average individual that this book is intended to reach (as opposed to security or law enforcement professionals, the opulently wealthy, or high-profile individuals with access to security options beyond the reach of most), there are dozens of simple, security measures described in these pages. While it's not possible to eliminate the possibility of victimization, you can reduce your odds.

Whether it's lighting, locks, alarms, surveillance, dogs or guns, don't rely on a single device or tactic to protect your property, yourself, or those you love. It is simply too easy to put multiple measures in place, and it's equally easy to ensure that you make active, ongoing use of those measures.

Index

A

B

C

V

vacation 97
  vacation security to-do list 97
valuables 101
  recording information 108
  what to store where 102
vehicles 97

W

windows 45
  adjacent to door locks 38
  alarm monitoring 47
  alarm sensors 69
  fire security 54
  garage 34
  glass security 52
  how to secure 47
  keyed sash locks 48
  pin locks / pinning 48
  reflective film 109
  second story 54
  security glass options 38, 52
  security screens / burglar bars 53
  types 45
    awning 46
    casement 45
    double hung 45
    jalousie 46
  unique concerns 52
    single hung 45

Y

yard
  address markers 77
  landscaping 76
  maintenance 98
  trash bins 76
  visibility issues 53

Notes:

Made in the USA
Middletown, DE
29 April 2025

74892926R00084